Oyo
Benin
Ashanti

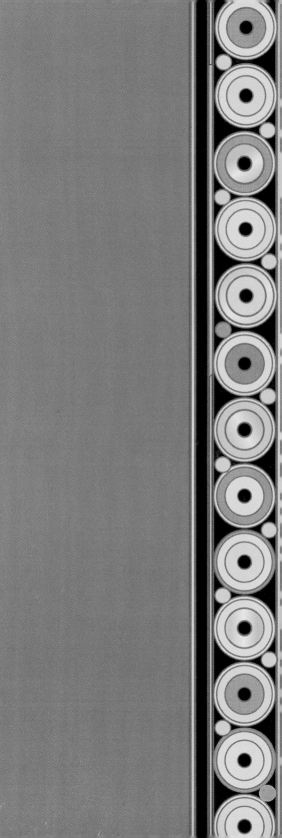

African Kingdoms of the Past

Oyo
Benin
Ashanti

•

The Guinea Coast

Kenny Mann

Dillon Press • Parsippany, New Jersey

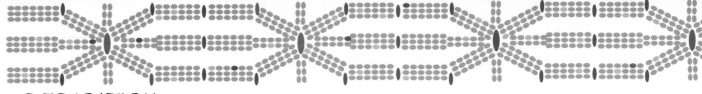

DEDICATION:
To Bettina, Don, Gabi, Gordian, Andrew, Victoria, Oliver, Jan, Richard, Orel, Jane, Nigel, Laura, Maria, and many other friends with thanks for their interest and support

ACKNOWLEDGMENTS
The author wishes to acknowledge the interest, patience and expertise of the following consultants:
Clarence G. Seckel, Jr., Curriculum Coordinator of Social Studies, School District 189, East St. Louis, IL; and Edna J. Whitfield, Social Studies Supervisor (retired), St. Louis Public Schools, MI.

CREDITS
Design and Illustration: Mary Ann Zanconato
Picture Research: Kenny Mann

PHOTO CREDITS
British Museum: 62, 63, Byron Crader/Root Resources: 85; Dirk Bakker: 15, 16; Foreign & Commonwealth Office: 29; Gerry Ellis Nature Photography: 38, 40-41; Joe Viesti/Viesti Associates: title, 42; John Elk III/ Bruce Coleman: 88-89; John Pemberton: 12; Metropolitan Museum of Art: Cover; Photograph by Eliot Elisofon National Museum of African Art, Eliot Elisofon Photographic Archives Smithsonian Institution: 75; Photograph by Henry J. Drewal The National Museum of African Art, Eliot Elisofon Photographic Archives, Smithsonian Institute: 25, 30; Photograph by Philip Gifford, American Museum of Natural History: 17; Royal Geographical Society: 53; S. Salgado/Magnum: 46; SBG: 39; Schomburg Center: 57, 66-67; The Nelson-Atkins Museum of Art: 80; Werner Forman Archive: 51; Maps, Ortelius Design: 4, 27, 55.

Library of Congress Cataloging-in-Publication Data
Mann, Kenny.
    Oyo, Benin, Ashanti : the Guinea coast / by Kenny Mann. — 1st ed.
    p. cm. — (African kingdoms of the past)
    Includes bibliographical references and index.
    ISBN 0-87518-657-2 — ISBN 0-382-39177-2 (pbk.)
    1. Guinea (Region)—History. I. Title. II. Series.
DT477.M36 1996   95-16060
966.52—dc20
Summary: A survey of the legends and history of the West African kingdoms of Oyo, Benin, and Ashanti, with discussion of the slave trade and its effect on the peoples of the Guinea Coast.

Copyright © 1996 by Kenny Mann

Published by Dillon Press,
A Division of Simon & Schuster,
299 Jefferson Road, Parsippany, NJ 07054

First edition
Printed in the United States of America
10 9 8 7 6 5 4 3 2 1

Table of Contents

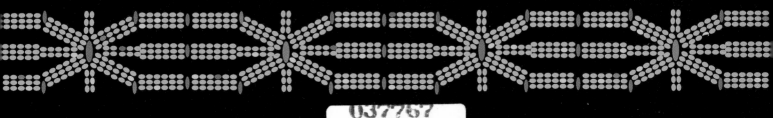

Introduction

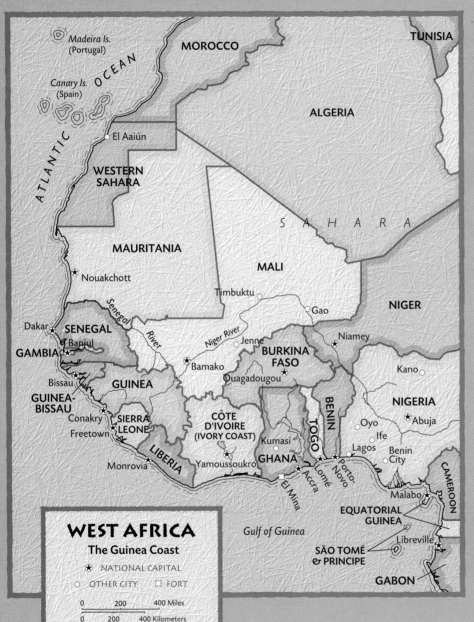

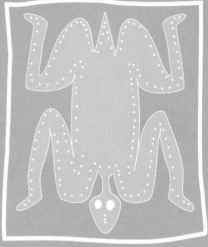

WEST AFRICA
The Guinea Coast

★ NATIONAL CAPITAL
○ OTHER CITY   ☐ FORT

| 0 | 200 | 400 Miles |
| 0 | 200 | 400 Kilometers |

Gambia, Guinea-Bissau, Guinea, Sierra Leone, Liberia, Ivory Coast, Ghana, Togo, Benin, and Nigeria—these are the nations of West Africa's Guinea (GIHN ee)* coast.

Today, big cities like Dakar (Senegal), Accra (Ghana), and Lagos (Nigeria) line the coast. They enjoy all the advantages of modern development: automobiles and airports; advanced telecommunications, school and health care systems; and recreational facilities such as golf courses. They also face all the problems common to big cities the world over: poverty, congestion, pollution, and crime.

The West African coastline is also dotted with ugly fortresses. These strongholds were built during the fifteenth and sixteenth centuries by European nations. They stand as a reminder of the 400-year-long trade in human beings that ravished certain areas of the Guinea coast and caused turmoil among its many peoples.

The slave trade began in the early sixteenth century, when Europeans first became familiar with the coastal regions. Exploration beyond the coast was difficult. There were few safe, natural harbors along the shore, and the river deltas, which offered entry to the rivers and to the interior, were lined with dank, mosquito-ridden mangrove swamps. Early traders were also intimidated by African leaders, who strictly controlled the movements of foreigners on their shores.

It was almost 400 years before the first Europeans penetrated the West African interior. There they found an abundance of valuable resources that they could exploit, including rare woods, foodstuffs, and minerals. European politicians, businessmen, and religious leaders all saw promise in the region. They could expand their empire, make huge profits in legitimate trade, and attempt to convert millions of Africans to Christianity. Although slavery gradually became less profitable, by the late nineteenth century, European interest in West Africa had mushroomed and was richly rewarded.

For most Africans, however, the nineteenth century was a time of violence and upheaval. No match for the European powers, they could only look on as their lands were carved up and portioned out among foreign powers, their valuable resources were exploited, and their traditional ways and beliefs were challenged. New nations, such as Ghana and Nigeria,

*Words that may be difficult to pronounce have been spelled phonetically in parentheses. A pronunciation key appears on page 93.

emerged. In the twentieth century many African states, including those of the Guinea coast, demanded independence from the European colonial powers and finally won it. Since the 1950s and 1960s, when many new, independent African nations emerged, Africans have had a new focus: to rebuild the African continent for Africans.

The focus on Africa elsewhere in the world has also shifted since the mid-twentieth century. Now, at last, non-Africans seem to be genuinely interested in learning more about the incredibly diverse peoples of Africa and their history. Of course, outsiders have always been fascinated by Africa. As early as the tenth century, Arab travelers who crossed the Sahara left behind vivid accounts of their journeys to the western Sudan, a region just north of the Guinea coastal region. They visited the great market cities that had arisen in the desert oases and along the Niger River, cities such as Kumbi, Timbuktu, and Jenne (JE ne). They described in detail the daily life of the people and the grandeur of the African kings' courts. Their accounts are important primary sources for historians today.

Few of these travelers reached the Guinea coast, however. For information about this region, historians and archaeologists must rely primarily on the written accounts of European traders and explorers from the late fifteenth century on. But they also turn to the oral histories of the Africans themselves. These stories, which have been told and retold over the centuries, are valuable sources of information.

The accuracy of both written and oral traditions depends, of course, on who is writing or telling the story. In the Middle Ages, for example, Arab authors often claimed that Arabs, not Africans, had founded the famous African dynasties. Oral historians sometimes bow to their sponsors, exaggerating the deeds of certain figures for posterity. Any historian, past

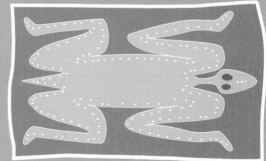

or present, may have a biased point of view.

History is not static. It changes as time goes on and new evidence is found. So our knowledge of the world also continues to change. When Europeans arrived on the coast of what is Ghana today, they called all Africans there Akan (AH kahn). Today, we know that many different, though related, cultural groups come under the Akan umbrella.

Not so long ago educated Africans, influenced by the European view-point, did not want to know about their ancestors because they considered them "primitive." But today, African scholars are in the forefront of such historical research. Together with foreign scholars they have been working to piece together the histories of the present-day African nations. The stories of Oyo (OH yoh), Benin (be NEEN), and Ashanti (ah-SHAHN tee) are part of the heritage of modern Ghana and Nigeria. Once great kingdoms, these places live on in the traditions, tales, and songs of the Nigerian and Ghanaian peoples.

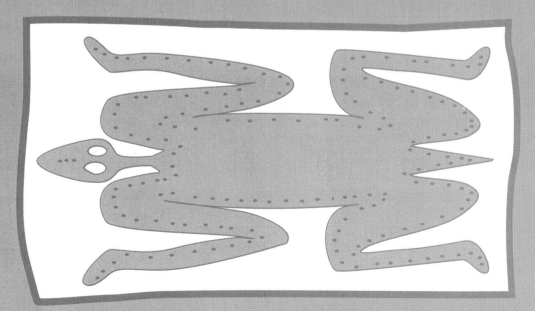

African Kingdoms

Note: Dates marked with an * are approximate.

| 4000 | B.C. | A.D. | 500 | 1200 | 1300 | 1400 |

*3500–2000 B.C. First written documents; Egypt establishes Old Kingdom

*500–350 B.C. Nok culture of central Nigeria developed

*A.D. 400–1000 Ghana develops into well-established kingdom along north-south trade routes across the Sahara. Origins of Yoruba states

570 Birth of Mohammed, founder of Islam

*1200 Sudanic pattern of development fully adapted in Guinea states

*1200–1300 Ife terra cottas made

1324–1325 Mansa Musa, king of Mali, makes his famous pilgrimage to Mecca

1375 First map of West Africa completed

*1440 Benin becomes powerful under Oba Ewuare

1471 Portuguese arrive on Guinea coast

1472 Ruy de Sequira first European to visit Benin

1482 El Mina built by Portuguese

1486 João d'Aveiro visits Benin

1492 Christopher Columbus arrives in the Americas

time

1500		**1800**		**2000**	

*1504 — D'Aveiro returns to Benin where Oba Esigie has just begun his long and successful reign

1532 — First shipload of African captives crosses the Atlantic

1591 — The Moroccans invade Songhay

*1650s — Firearms become increasingly important weapon in Africa

*1690s–1800 — Ashanti kingdom founded by Osei Tutu; kingdom expands to include most of modern Ghana

1726–1730 — Oyo kingdom at peak of power

*1750 — Slave trade at its peak

1776 — United States declares independence from Great Britain

1804 — Usuman dan Fodio attacks Oyo; Napoleon I becomes Emperor of France

1805–1817 — Slave trade abolished by European nations and the United States

1814 — First steam engine developed in England

1826 — British Royal Navy captain Hugh Clapperton first European to visit Oyo

1834–1865 — Slavery abolished in British and French colonies and the United States

1873 — British capture Kumasi, defeat Ashanti

1884 — The imperial powers claim African territories at the Berlin Congress

1897 — British expedition reaches Benin

1902 — British Colony and protectorate of the Gold Coast formed

1910-1911 — Ife terra-cotta and bronze heads seen by Frobenius; Gold Coast (Ghana) experiences boom in cocoa export

1914 — British Colony and Protectorate of Nigeria formed; start of World War I

1931 — Nok terra-cotta heads found by tin miners

1933 — Adolph Hitler heads fascist government in Germany

1939–1945 — World War II

1957 — Gold Coast gains independence and is renamed Ghana

1960 — Nigeria gains independence

Ife—City of Light

Oduduwa Descends from the Sky Kingdom

At the very beginning of time, before there were people on the earth, the Great Creator Olodumare (oh loh doo-MAH ray) reigned in the sky. He was the Supreme Being, the owner of everything and creator of the sky.

Olodumare was not alone. With him, up there in the sky, dwelled many other lesser gods, or *orishas* (oh REE shuhz), as they were called. Among these was Orunmila (oh ROON mee lah), who could foretell the future. There was Oduduwa (oh DOO doo wah), one of Olodumare's most trusted *orishas*. And there was Obatala (oh bah TAH lah), the Supreme Being's son.

Below the sky, the goddess Olokun (oh loh KOON) ruled over the gray waters where there was no life, neither plant nor animal. And thus the two kingdoms existed, each ruled by its gods.

One day, Oduduwa looked down upon the watery kingdom below. "How gray and lifeless it is," he thought to himself. "How colorless! Surely, it should be filled with living things. I could arrange this."

So Oduduwa asked Olodumare for permission to create land, and it was given. First, Oduduwa went to Orunmila, who could foretell the future, and asked for his advice. Orunmila brought out his divining tray and cast sixteen palm nuts on it. Again and again he cast the nuts upon the tray, and when at last he had divined their meaning, he said to Oduduwa, "Here is what you must do. Go down to the watery wastes below on a chain of gold. Take with you a snail shell full of sand, a white hen, a palm nut, and a black cat to be your companion."

So Oduduwa took a great golden chain and fastened its hook to the edge of the sky. Then, carefully carrying the snail shell, the hen, the palm nut, and the cat, he slowly climbed down the chain. When he reached the end of the chain, Oduduwa realized that it was not long enough. There he was, precariously dangling above the empty expanse of water! He clung to the chain in fear.

Suddenly, Oduduwa heard Orunmila calling from above. "Pour out the sand!" he cried. So Oduduwa poured the sand from the snail shell. Then he heard Orunmila's voice say, "The hen!" Oduduwa dropped the hen onto the sand. At once, the hen began scratching away. The sand flew in all directions, forming hills and valleys and plains wherever it landed.

Now Oduduwa was able to drop down from the chain and walk on this land. He named the place where he landed Ife (EE fe) and built a house there. Then he planted the palm nut, and from it a palm tree grew, and from the seeds of that tree grew many more palm trees. And for a long, long time, Oduduwa lived at Ife, with only his cat for company.

After a time, the great god Olodumare wished to know how things were progressing down below. So he sent his messenger, Agemo (ah GE moh) the chameleon, to descend the golden chain and see what was going on. "Things are going very well," Oduduwa told him. "But it is too gray. There should be more light." And Agemo carried this message back to Olodumare, who created the sun and set it in motion. Thus there was light and warmth on earth.

Now Obatala, Olodumare's son, became interested in Ife and the new kingdom below. From his father, the Supreme Being, he received permission to join Oduduwa, and so he left the sky kingdom and lived in Ife. But after some time, Obatala grew lonely. He had only Oduduwa to talk to! Obatala decided to create people. He dug clay from the ground and fashioned it into human shapes. The Supreme Being Olodumare breathed into them, and they came alive. Oduduwa gave each person a wooden hoe and a copper bush knife, and the people began to grow millet and yams. They built houses and multiplied, and Ife became a large and prosperous city.

Oduduwa became the first king, or *oni* (OH nee), of Ife and ruled the people. Obatala resented this and began a rebellion, but he was driven out of the city. He traveled far and became the ruler of another group of people. Oduduwa was the ancestor of a great dynasty. His children—there were sixteen of them—received crowns and spread from Ife all over the land to found new kingdoms, among them the great kingdom of Benin.

For this reason had the soothsayer Orunmila used sixteen palm nuts in his divining tray. And in this way were the kingdoms of the Yoruba (YOH roo buh) created, and Oduduwa was seen as the "father" of all the Yoruba people. And the city of Ife was known as "the center of the world, whence came the light."

◀ After Ododuwa founded Ife, he gave a beaded crown much like this one to each of the sixteen princes who left the city to found new Yoruba kingdoms. The Yoruba believe that when the crown is placed upon a king's head it unites his "inner head" with all those who have gone before him and who are now *orishas*. The long-tailed royal bird, Okin, adorns each crown.

The Origins of the Yoruba

The homeland of the Yoruba today stretches from the swampy coast of Nigeria across the misty gloom of the tropical forest to the woodland bush and park-like savanna south of the Niger River's great bend. About the size of England, it is mostly a fertile land, watered by many streams and rivers.

The Yoruba have occupied this land for many centuries. But little is known about their origins and early history. In the languages of the neighboring Hausa (HOU zuh) and Fulani (foo LAH nee) peoples, the word *yoruba* means "cunning." Perhaps, centuries ago, there were reasons for this name. There were many Yoruba kingdoms at that time, and fierce rivalry arose between the Yoruba city-states. Today, however, the Yoruba think of themselves as one people drawn together by a common language and rich culture, with its spiritual center at Ife.

The legend of Oduduwa and the other *orishas* explains that the ancestors of the Yoruba came down from the sky and founded the city of Ife. Of course, there are no written records that document this event. In fact, there are no written records at all of Yoruba history until the late fifteenth century, when European traders arrived on the Guinea coast. Having no written language, the Yoruba, like most other African peoples, entrusted

Deities of the Yoruba

The Yoruba believe in some 400 greater and lesser gods, or *orishas*, whom they revere to this day. These gods are deeply involved in human affairs as well as their own. They have many human characteristics and may be good or evil, wise or stupid, and even unpredictable. The Yoruba do not judge the behavior of their gods. They are simply accepted as forces of nature.

The Yoruba gods include

Agemo—the chameleon; not an *orisha*, but Olodumare's messenger

Eshu—*orisha* of chance

Obatala—son of Olodumare and creator of people

Oduduwa—father of the Yoruba and founder of Ife

Olodumare—owner of the sky, Supreme Being, Creator

Olokun—female *orisha* of the sea

Oranyan—founder of Oyo, father of Shango

Orunmila—the *orisha* of divination

Oya and Oshun—Shango's wives, *orishas* of the Niger and Oshun rivers.

Shango—son of Oranyan and *orisha* of thunder and lightning

their history to the memory of special individuals called *aroken* (ah ROH ken). Much like the *griots* (gree OHZ) of other West African regions, these men handed down the tribal legends and stories from one generation to the next.

While the *aroken*s' accounts differ somewhat in detail, the basic story remains the same. In some versions, for example, Oduduwa came down from the sky kingdom already accompanied by sixteen companions. One of these was Obatala, who quarreled with Oduduwa and went off to found his own kingdom.

Because it mentions sand and palm trees, the founding story

◄ This bronze portrait of an Ife king, or *oni*, was cast in the thirteenth century. In his left hand he carries a horn; in his right hand he carried an ax. Both are symbols of power.

This terra-cotta head, found at Nok, was made between 500 B.C. and A.D. 200. ▶

has led scholars to believe that the Yoruba were not originally forest people. But even so, the question of the Yoruba's actual origins remains open to speculation. In the early nineteenth century, a historian from the Sudan claimed that during biblical times the Yoruba had been driven out of the country known today as Iraq and traveled westward from there. In 1897 another historian wrote that Oduduwa was in fact a son of Lamurudu, one of the kings of Mecca. Mecca is the holy city of the Muslim faith. It lies on the east bank of the Red Sea, in Saudi Arabia.

In 1955 a Nigerian historian suggested that the Yoruba migrated from the kingdom of Meroë (ME roh), also known as the Land of Kush (koosh), between A.D. 600 and 1000. Meroë was located along the west bank of the middle Nile, near present-day Khartoum. Today, the Yoruba themselves favor this idea. They believe that the people described in medieval

This bronze head, found in Benin, was cast between 1550 and 1680. In real life the hat, pendants, and necklaces were made of valuable red coral beads. ▶

Arabic records as "the sons of Kush, who marched toward the setting sun" are their ancestors.

There is a good deal of support for this theory. The national god of the Yoruba is Shango (shan GOH), who is worshipped with a ram's-head mask. The coiled serpent, made of clay, wood, or metal, is also a popular symbol among the Yoruba. Similar masks and serpents have been found in the ruins of Meroë. The political structure of Yoruba society (which will be discussed later) may also have been modeled on that of ancient Kush and its neighbor, Egypt. Some scholars also believe that the Yoruba language is similar to that of ancient Egypt.

Whatever their origins, it is certain that the Yoruba were living in what is today western Nigeria and had founded the city of Ife by the ninth century. It is also known that some time after Oduduwa arrived in Ife, the many princes of his clan spread out over the land to found new Yoruba kingdoms and dynasties. No one really knows why the clan scattered. Some believe there was a terrible drought that forced the Yoruba in Ife to seek better lands. Others have suggested that Ife was so prosperous that the population increased rapidly, placing too much pressure on the available resources. And some say that the companions from the sky kingdom quarreled, and many chose to leave.

Oduduwa is still honored by millions of the Yoruba people as a god, the emissary (agent or representative) of the Supreme Being. He is seen as the symbol of Yoruba unity, as the ancestor of all Yoruba everywhere, and as the first king of Ife. Obatala is also still worshipped as a great god and as the creator of people. His festival is one of the most important events of the year in Ife. Ife itself still exists, located about 320 km (200 mi) northeast of Lagos, in the belt of dense forest that hugs the Guinea coast. Present-day Ife is believed to stand near or on its original site. It is still revered as the spiritual home of the Yoruba, the center of their universe and the cradle of their culture.

Clues to the Nation's History

In 1897 a British expedition reached the city of Benin—not to be confused with the modern nation of Benin—320 km (200 mi) southeast of Ife. There the British found an extraordinary collection of bronze masks, plaques, figures, and other artifacts. Tradition in Benin says that the art of bronze casting was brought there from Ife. But the Europeans could not believe that "primitive" Africans had produced such beautiful and finely crafted art, and the origin of the bronze work remained a mystery to early European historians.

In the early 1900s a German anthropologist named Leo Frobenius (froh-BAY nee us) made further impressive discoveries while investigating the sacred shrines of Ife. The Yoruba people showed Frobenius a magnificent bronze head of the goddess of the sea, Olokun. Frobenius also collected exquisite terra-cotta heads of men and women and recorded the many stone monuments he found in the town. Then he announced to the world, offering no proof whatsoever, that the

works he had found at Ife had been made by Greek artists from the legendary lost continent of Atlantis!

Frobenius's reports caused great excitement among scholars in Europe and led to many other finds. In the 1930s, Europeans still doubted that these works of art, which ranked alongside those of ancient Greece and Rome, could have been created by Africans. It was even suggested that they had been made by the Portuguese, who sailed to the Guinea coast in the late fifteenth century. After World War II, however, the new technology of carbon dating placed the Ife terra cottas at about A.D. 1200–1300, nearly 300 years before the Portuguese arrived in West Africa. The Benin artwork was dated between the fifteenth and sixteenth centuries, after the arrival of the Portuguese. No connections at all could be established between the traditional art of the Portuguese and that of the Benin people.

Meanwhile, in 1931, tin miners near the village of Nok, in central Nigeria, unearthed two red-clay heads, slightly less than life-sized. It was a small find,

to be sure, but one that would eventually provide some clues to the Yoruba's past.

Over the years, hundreds of Nok figurines have been found over an area some 480 km (300 mi) wide. The sculptures are realistic, clearly showing clothing, tribal marks, jewelry, weapons, and other details. Figures from other parts of Africa are usually much more symbolic and less detailed. It has been determined that the Nok heads were made sometime between 500 and 350 B.C. But we still know very little about the Nok culture, and whether it was, in fact, connected to the Yoruba people.

Many centers of bronze casting have now been found throughout the lands inhabited by the Yoruba. In fact, bronze casting is still done in some places. As more works of art are discovered, historians are better able to piece together scraps and patches of Yoruba history. Many questions remain, however. Did the people of Benin—the Bini (BEE nee)—and those of Ife learn their craft from artists in Nok? What was the purpose of the sculptures? Did they represent kings and gods? Or were some of them family portraits? Did the art flourish at Ife before or after the arrival of Oduduwa and his companions? Was it made there, or brought there by outsiders? Without answers to these questions, we can only marvel at the technical knowledge required to produce such works of art. The people who made them must have been highly skilled professional artists, possibly commissioned and paid by the king or other wealthy individuals. And only a highly organized, politically stable society could afford such artisans.

Oyo—Golden Age of the Yoruba

Shango Confronts His Jealousy

When the people left Ife to start new dynasties, the *orisha* called Oranyan (oh RAHN yahn) traveled far to the north, looking for a place to start a town. At last he found a suitable hill for his settlement. He built a town there and named it Oyo (OH yoh), which means "slippery place," because his horse had stumbled there.

In time, after Oranyan's death, his son Shango became the king, or *oba* (OH bah), of Oyo. Shango ruled sternly over the city and all the lands around it. He was the god of thunder and lightning, and his anger struck terror into the hearts of his subjects. His double-bladed ax showed that his power reached all the corners of the kingdom. No one could escape his wrath.

Shango's armies conquered one nation after another until Oyo was the most powerful of them all. Among the brave warriors who had fought for Shango were two men named Timi (TEE mee) and Gbonka (guh BON kah). They were famed throughout Oyo for their bravery in battle. Everywhere the warriors went, their drummers beat out their praise songs.

Timi and Gbonka were much loved among the people, and in time, Shango became jealous of them. With an evil heart, he plotted to get rid of them.

First, Shango ordered Timi to go to the city of Ede (AY day), many miles to the south. "The people there have forgotten that I am their master and they are my servants," Shango said. "You must subdue them and be their leader."

Timi took his bow and the flaming arrows he used in war. He adorned his body with talismans, or charms, for good luck and mounted his horse. With a few warrior companions, he rode off to Ede.

"Good," thought Shango. "He will surely be killed in battle against the Ede."

But Timi and his men defeated the Ede, and Timi became their king. In time the city of Ede became rich and powerful. When Shango heard this, jealousy ate again at his heart, and he vowed to rid himself of Timi forever. He called the mighty warrior Gbonka to his palace. "Your friend Timi swore to subdue Ede," he said, "but that place is now vain and proud and has forgotten who is its true master! You will go there to defeat Timi and bring him back here to me."

Gbonka remembered how he and Timi had fought side by side in the bloodiest battles of Oyo. "I cannot fight Timi, Great Master," he said, "for he is my brother. One of us will surely die."

Now this is exactly what Shango intended. So he commanded Gbonka to go to Ede.

Sadly, Gbonka hung his body with medicine bundles and talismans. He took an antelope horn in which he kept the most powerful of his magic charms, or *jujus* (JOO jooz). Then he mounted his horse and rode to Ede.

The meeting between Timi and Gbonka was like that of two brothers, for indeed they had been comrades in war and did not wish to fight. But Gbonka could not persuade Timi to return with him to Oyo. "Shango sent me here, and here I shall stay," Timi insisted. "In that case," replied Gbonka, "I must bring you by force."

The warriors' drummers beat out their lords' praise songs to announce the duel. Timi placed a flaming arrow in his bow. But Gbonka raised only his medicine horn and with a magic spell put Timi instantly to sleep.

Gbonka lay Timi gently over a horse and brought him back to Oyo, as Shango had commanded. But Shango was even more troubled, because both warriors were now back in the city. Yet again, he plotted their deaths.

Shango knew that Timi was humiliated. The people taunted him, saying that he had fallen asleep in the face of battle. "You are a fool!" Shango said to Timi. "How can you let the people laugh at you like this? You must fight Gbonka again, and defeat him."

Timi had lost all his power as the king of Ede, and he hated to be ridiculed. His heart raced for revenge against his former comrade in arms. That same day, the royal criers ran through the city, announcing a battle between the two warriors.

Timi and Gbonka faced each other in the royal compound. Their drummers beat out their praise songs. Timi released a flaming arrow from his mighty bow, but Gbonka raised his medicine horn and the arrow flew to the east. The next arrow flew to the west. And when all the arrows were gone, Gbonka chanted his magic spell and Timi fell to the ground in a deep sleep.

Shango was furious. Fire spurted from his mouth and the trees shook with his rage. "To the death!" he shouted. "Fight to the death!"

Now Gbonka was also enraged. "Twice have I fought my comrade for you!" he shouted. "I will do as you wish, Great Master, but when Timi is dead, you will have to deal with me. Either you or I will leave Oyo forever."

Once again, the drummers beat out their masters' praise songs. Shango watched from his throne as the warriors faced each other, calling out taunts and jibes. Once again, Timi loosed his flaming arrows. And again, Gbonka's magic spell caused Timi to fall to the ground in deep sleep. But this time, Gbonka raised his sword and severed Timi's head with one blow.

Gbonka threw Timi's bleeding head into Shango's lap. "You have what you wanted!" he bellowed. Shango's eyes blazed red with anger. With a roar, he ordered his soldiers to burn Gbonka at the stake. But Gbonka would not burn. He stood among the flames, staring at Shango. In terror, the people fled. What had the gods brought among them now? Shango opened his mouth and aimed a tongue of flame at Gbonka. But the steel-eyed warrior remained unharmed.

Gbonka could not be conquered. This Shango understood. In shame he departed from Oyo forever. It is said that Shango hung himself from a tree. But it is also said that he returned to the sky kingdom, to resume his duties as the *orisha* of thunder and lightning.

The Yoruba today still practice many traditional rituals. Here, a worshipper of Shango carries a Shango "dance wand" in a procession. The shape at the top represents Shango's thunderbolts.

Recollections of the Past

In all ancient Yoruba legends, the kings and heroes are portrayed as gods. Did they really exist? As is the case with all legends, there is probably some truth in each story. Shango, for example, was not only the *orisha* of thunder and lightning, but also a king, a warrior, and a magician. There are many stories about him. Today, the Yoruba still honor Shango and the many *orishas* of the legends with festivals and prayers.

Historians believe that after Shango's reign, Yoruba history moves out of the realm of legend and into that of real memory. The Yoruba storytellers, or *aroken*, have preserved the names of many kings of Oyo as well as the accounts of some of their exploits.

At one time, the *aroken* tell us, Oyo was attacked by the Nupe (NOO pe), hostile neighbors of the Oyo who

lived across the Niger, just 30 or 40 miles to the northeast. When the Nupe attacked, the king had to flee. His departure from Oyo marked the beginning of a long period of exile for the Oyo kings and their followers. When, after many years, a later king decided to return to Oyo, he was attacked by the Borgu (bor GOO), enemies of the Oyo who lived to the northwest. But a clever Oyo warrior who was also a woodcarver hatched a plan. He made lifelike models of archers for the Oyo to place in the bush to fool the Borgu. In this way the king and his followers were able to cover their escape.

Another king also tried to return to Oyo. On his way he came upon a place where two streams flowed together. The omens were good, so the king founded a new capital there. The city was called Oyo Igboho (OH yoh ig BOH hoh), and the Oyo kings reigned there for many years. Igboho was famed for its three great earthen ramparts, which can still be seen today. According to tradition, one of its rulers was a woman who command-ed a formidable army.

In one episode, Igboho was attacked by the Nupe, and the Oyo soldiers could not push them back. A brave Oyo warrior named Ajanlapa (ah jahn-LA pah) dressed in the king's clothes and drew the enemy line of fire. His body was immediately pierced by thousands of arrows and spears. The shafts held Ajanlapa's body upright, his teeth transfixed in a hideous grin. Thinking that what they saw was a spirit, the enemy fled in terror.

The last king of Igboho was deter-mined to return to Oyo and sent a party of soldiers ahead to scout out the city. His nobles, however, did not want to leave their farms and houses, and so devised a trick. A group of people hurried ahead to Oyo and disguised themselves as terrifying spirits. When the soldiers arrived, they were confronted by grotesque creatures who waved torches and shrieked: *"Ko si aiye, ko si aiye!"* (koh see EYE yay)—"No room, no room!" The soldiers ran for their lives. But the king discov-ered the trick and eventually did return to Oyo. The city remained the capital of the kingdom for many centuries.

From City to Kingdom

The city of Oyo was far—about 320 km (200 mi)—from Ife on the northern edge of the Yoruba lands. At first, Oyo was not very important. But by about the fourteenth century, it had become a major power in the north. By the mid-eighteenth century, Oyo commanded a kingdom that stretched almost 800 km (500 mi) from the coast to the Niger bend and was more than 480 km (300 mi) wide in some places.

How could such an insignificant city have developed into such a large kingdom? The city's location seems to have been a significant factor in its development. A low range of rocky

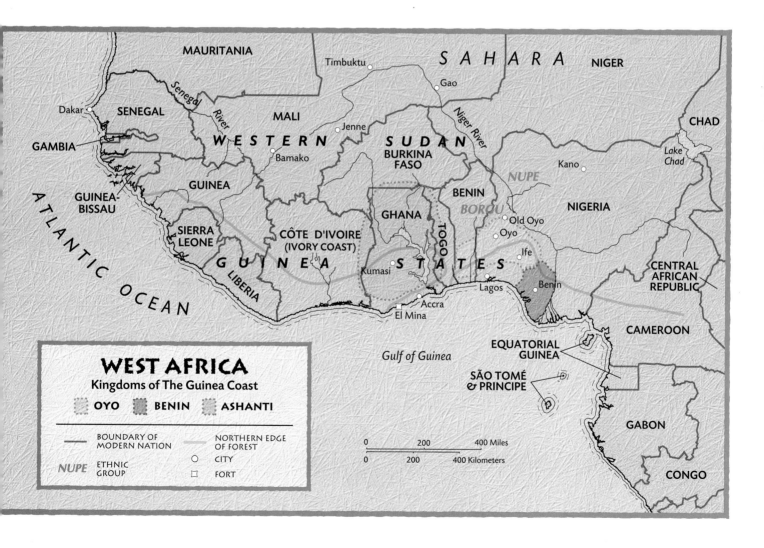

The strength and size of the Oyo army was legendary. According to the Dahomeans, when the Oyo went to war, their general spread a thick buffalo hide before his tent. On either side, he placed a spear. His soldiers marched between the spears. When they had worn a hole in the hide, the general assumed that he had enough forces to take the field. How many men, and how many hours, would this take? No one really knows.

hills along its western flank formed a natural defense against enemies. In addition, open grasslands surrounded the city. Here the Oyo could raise cattle, sheep, and goats. They could also keep horses for their cavalry, which was a vital part of the Oyo army. Most other Yoruba lands lay within the dense forests along the Guinea coast. The forest dwellers were unable to keep horses, cattle, or other pack animals because of the tsetse (TSE tsee) fly, whose bite transmits a deadly disease. For this reason, warfare in the forest regions generally took place on foot. The Oyo's cavalry alone gave them a huge advantage over the foot soldiers of the south.

Oyo also lay conveniently close to trade routes that ran from the southern forests across the Niger River to the marketplaces of the western Sudan. Thus the people of Oyo were in close contact with non-Yoruba peoples to the north, including the Hausa as well as the Borgu and Nupe. The Hausa traded with Arab merchants who traveled from the North African coast across the Sahara to the western Sudan. These traders brought not only goods but also new political, military, and technical ideas to the lands south of the Sahara. Goods and ideas came first to Oyo, and through it to other Yoruba lands. The city of Oyo thus developed into a lively and prosperous center of trade. After the sixteenth century, the Oyo people also became heavily involved in the export of slaves to the Americas.

In the course of four centuries, the Oyo kings waged war after war with their neighbors. First they overcame the Nupe and Borgu. Then they conquered Yoruba lands to the south. The southeast remained invincible, protected by the armies of the neighboring kingdom of Benin. But between 1726 and 1730, the Oyo took huge areas in the southwest, penetrating deep into the neighboring kingdom of Dahomey (dah hoh mee).

Wood and stone for building are scarce in West Africa. Many villages and cities are built of red mud or brick, which can wash away in the rains. Few traces are left of some of the magnificent buildings described by early travelers to Oyo. In 1826 the British navy captain Hugh Clapperton wrote, "The people . . . are fond of ornamenting their doors and the posts which support their verandahs, with carvings . . . principally of the boa snake, with a hog or antelope in its mouth; frequently of men taking slaves. . . ." Similar details are evident in this door from the palace at Oyo. ▶

Male elders of the Ogboni (og BOH nee) council, which also has female members, are responsible for the selection, installation, removal (if necessary), and burial of kings. They also judge criminals. ▼

At this time, according to the oral tradition, the Oyo kingdom covered about 26,000 sq. km (10,000 sq. mi).

The first half of the eighteenth century was Oyo's "golden age of conquest." But, like other kingdoms that grew too large to govern effectively, Oyo was bound, in the end, to fall.

Yoruba Government

There were many cities in the Yoruba lands, each surrounded by its state and each ruled by an *oba*, or king. The Oyo kingdom consisted of several such city-states. The city of Ife was the most important of these because it was the Yoruba's spiritual and cultural center.

Captured kingdoms or states had to pay large sums of money, or tributes, to the Oyo. The Yoruba developed a many-layered system of government to control these areas. They determined boundaries between kingdoms and distributed power carefully.

At the head of government was the *alafin* (ah LAH feen). The *alafin* ruled over the huge expanse of the Yoruba lands and over all the *obas* of the city-states in the kingdom. In his palace, the *alafin* was attended by many hundreds of officials, priests, musicians, and servants. There were high officials who represented the *alafin* at court, in religious ceremonies, and in administrative and military functions. Then there were 68 royal slaves. Each bore a special title reflecting the *alafin*'s intentions, such as *oba ko she tan* (OH bah koh shay tan), or "the king is not ready." This royal bodyguard also supervised government in other cities. The *alafin*'s "special agents," who were located throughout the country, were called the *asoju oba* (ah SOH joo OH bah) or "the eyes of the king." The Ogboni society, a secret but influential cult, ensured that the *alafin* received the powers of

his ancestors. The *alafin*'s official mother, the *iya oba* (EE yuh OH bah), led the women of the palace, who were also extremely powerful. Among them were wives, officials, priestesses, and royal slaves.

European records from the late nineteenth century tell us much abut the pomp and ceremony at the *alafin*'s palace. At his coronation, the *alafin* received a special beaded crown, which was said to have come from Oduduwa, the first ancestor of the Yoruba. Thereafter, the *alafin* appeared in public at only three special festivals of the year. Otherwise he rarely left the palace, except to take a secret stroll on moonlit nights.

Because the *alafin*'s office was sacred, his well-being affected the well-being of his people. The *alafin* appointed all local chiefs and controlled the use of all land belonging to the city. His authority and power, however, went much further. The *alafin* was usually the wealthiest man in the kingdom, since tributes from member states and tolls at the city's gates and markets were paid to him.

The *Oba's* People

Yoruba society was organized into clans, or groups that claimed descent from one ancestor. These people usually lived together in their own section of a town, called a ward or *adugbo* (ah DOOG boh). There were sometimes 1,000 or more people in one ward.

All Yoruba people lived in or had close ties to a parent town. All were also farmers, sharing in the cultivation of family land. Many practiced various crafts and trades, such as weaving and ironworking. Pottery making and cloth dying were reserved for women. Sometimes, whole families specialized in certain crafts and were organized into guilds and protected by their own gods. People also belonged to various "age sets," depending on when they were born. Each age set had specific rights and duties.

The Yoruba employed many slaves, mostly as farm laborers, servants, bodyguards, and traders. In royal households, slaves could be ambassadors or hold other important posts. They were allowed to own property and to cultivate their own land. Until about 1790 most slaves were non-Yoruba prisoners of war. After that date, many native Yoruba were captured by their own chiefs for sale to coastal traders.

He was the supreme judge in all Yoruba appeals, and the only person who could declare war.

Though the *alafin's* power was impressive, it was not unlimited. Like any Yoruba *oba*, the *alafin* had to submit his decisions to a council of seven honored men, the Oyo Mesi (OH yoh ME see). Their leader, the Bashorun (bah SHOH roon), was even more powerful than they. Through his divinations, the Bashorun chose who was to be the *alafin*.

If the *alafin* was a good and wise man, he could often initiate and carry through policies. He could even overrule the Oyo Mesi when they opposed him. But if the *alafin* was foolish or strong-willed, the Oyo Mesi would send him a gift of parrot's eggs—a polite way of inviting him to commit suicide by taking poison.

The Oyo Mesi also ruled that an *alafin*'s eldest son had to end his life upon his father's death. This prevented any ambitious young princes from competing for power with the local *obas*. The *alafin*'s mother also had to "go to sleep" when her son became king. She could produce no more sons with rights to the throne.

The palaces of other Yoruba *obas*, and even of the lesser chiefs of small settlements, were run much like the *alafin*'s palace, though on a less grand scale.

Outside the *alafin*'s palace—but well connected at all levels of government—special groups of chiefs were responsible for war, trade, hunting, law, order, and justice. In most Yoruba towns, the women were represented by an influential female chief, selected by the *oba*. She took part in the political business of the state and coordinated the women's activities.

Government and daily life among the Yoruba was highly structured and controlled. But in many ways the Yoruba had created a fairly democratic constitution with many checks and balances to power. Although these varied in detail from place to place, the main features of the government—the town, its *oba*, the hierarchy of chiefs and priests with their various responsibilities— were found everywhere.

The Fall of Oyo

On January 23, 1826, Captain Hugh Clapperton of the British Royal Navy became the first European to set foot in Oyo. He had traveled for 47 days by canoe, on horseback, and on foot, following the main Oyo trade route from the coast.

To Clapperton the Oyo towns, markets, farms, and family compounds seemed peaceful and prosperous and firmly under the control of the current *alafin*. But all was not well in the kingdom.

When Clapperton arrived in Oyo, the slave trade, which had been going on for nearly 400 years, was still in full force. But various kings and ambitious individuals were in deadly competition for its control. Tensions were rising. Moreover, as the kingdom grew to include the forest belt along the coast, there were more resources for the Oyo conquerors to plunder. This, too, caused competition where there had once been unity.

Historians believe that these tensions upset the balance of power between the *alafin*, the Oyo Mesi, and other government leaders. Several *alafins* were forced to commit suicide by the Oyo Mesi. One *alafin* reigned for only three months! This lack of support for the *alafin* damaged the traditional structure of government and the spiritual beliefs of the people.

These were some of the internal problems of the kingdom. External factors also had an effect on life there.

In the last half of the eighteenth century, the Nupe, Borgu, and Egba (EG buh) territories went to war against the *alafin* and broke away from the kingdom. The army lost its main suppliers of horses, which had always come from the Nupe and other areas north of the Niger. Without a cavalry, the army was ineffective.

In the early 1800s, a Muslim religious leader named Usuman dan Fodio (OO zu mahn dahn foh dee oh)

Islam

Islam was founded in the seventh century by the prophet Mohammed, who was born in Mecca in A.D. 571. Through a series of dreamlike visions, he was led to the ideas and founding rules of a new religion he called Islam. The word means "submission," and those who submit to the one god, Allah, are called Muslims. Mecca has been the holy city of Islam since A.D. 630. The holy book of Islam is the Quran (koh RAHN), or Koran.

By the mid-eighteenth century, the Muslims had conquered Egypt, Syria, Iraq, and most of North Africa. Lured by the legendary gold of ancient Ghana, and later of other kingdoms, Muslims invaded West Africa several times. Early invaders forced those they conquered to convert to Islam. They were followed by more peaceful Muslim merchants and travelers, who introduced Arab learning in science, mathematics, medicine, architecture, and geography. Muslims founded universities in Jenne, Timbuktu, and other West African towns. Arabic, the written language of the Muslims, was used to record African chronicles, which had been handed down orally for centuries. These early written records have been invaluable resources for historians.

Today, about 50 percent of Nigerians and 10 percent of Ghanaians are Muslim. About 40 percent of people in both countries are Christian. Only 10 percent of Nigerians, but 45 percent of Ghanaians, practice traditional beliefs.

conquered Hausaland, to the north of Oyo. Determined to spread the Islamic religion throughout the Yoruba lands as well, Usuman led his army in a holy war or *jihad* (JEE- hahd) against the Yoruba. The Muslims captured a town near Oyo, cutting off the capital from the rest of the kingdom. They raided and destroyed many other Oyo towns. The city of Oyo was abandoned, and thousands of refugees fled south, seeking safety in the forest.

Meanwhile, in 1818, the Dahomeans to the west had refused to pay tribute to Oyo, and their armies were sweeping through the southern Yoruba lands. In the east, the kingdom of Benin was pushing ever westward. And in the south, the British had claimed the port of Lagos and would soon push north.

Oyo was more or less squeezed out of existence. For a time, a new king-dom called Ibadan (ih BAH dahn) flourished. But by 1914 the British had asserted their power and forced a shaky peace on the many warring factions of the land. The British Colony and Protectorate of Nigeria was born. It included not only the Yoruba, but also the Hausa, Igbo (EEG boh), and many other non-Yoruba peoples.

The Yoruba were influenced now by Christian missionaries and Western culture and education. For almost 50 years, until Nigeria won its independence from Great Britain in 1960, they had to bend to an entirely new kind of government. In the long history of the Yoruba people, 50 years of colonial rule was but a tiny fraction of time. For centuries the Yoruba— the "children of Oduduwa"—have kept their stories and traditions alive. Who knows what the future may bring for these proud people?

The Building of Kingdoms

Long before the Portuguese arrived on the shores of West Africa they had a name for the lands they had heard of only in fables. They called West Africa "Guinea," which was a shortened form of the Berber term *Akal en Iguinawen* (ah kahl en ih GIHN ah-wen), the "land of the blacks." Today, the name Guinea refers to the countries along West Africa's southern coast.

Once Portuguese sailors had rounded the "bulge" of West Africa, they faced a daunting task—to anchor safely beyond the surf that pounds the massive rocks of the Guinea shore. White spray from the breakers shoots up as high as the palm trees. The Europeans thought the spray was steam—convincing proof, they said, that the rivers of Africa were made of fire.

The European sailors needed the help of skilled African canoers to bring them in to land. Some crew members, however, might have preferred to stay on board ship, for the Guinea shores are not particularly inviting. The sailors had to work their way through the lagoons and creeks of Dahomey and along the coasts of the Oyo kingdom. Here, gloomy mangrove swamps line the dark, brackish waters. From May to October, the

Trading was vigorous between villages on the river deltas. Many goods, such as livestock, foodstuffs, ivory, gold, and slaves, were transported in long, graceful trading canoes. They held 20 or more men and were also used to transport soldiers in times of war.

air is moist and steamy, and rain pours from leaden skies. From November to February, it is cooler and drier. But the *harmattan* (HAHR mah tan) winds from the north blow mercilessly, clouding the skies with dust from the Sahara. Mosquitoes and other disease-carrying bugs plagued the Portuguese, and many died. The Guinea coast went down in history as "the white man's grave."

Despite their hardships the Portuguese, and other Europeans who followed them, set up trading posts along the West African shores. But few of them ventured inland. Only much later did they realize that the swamps were actually the

At low tide the mangrove roots are exposed in black, stinking mud.

People living in the forest regions developed extensive trade networks connecting their many villages, towns, and cities. Mahogany, teak, ebony, and silk-cotton trees are valuable forest resources.

deltas of several navigable rivers that emptied into the Atlantic.

The deltas are backed by a strip of flat land, from 3 to 80 km (2 to 50 mi) wide, that is covered with grass and low scrub. Beyond this plain is the deep forest extending 320 km (200 mi) into the interior. Mahogany trees there tower 70 m (200 ft) above the ground. Below them, teak, ebony, and silk-cotton trees stretch toward the light, their leaves dripping with moisture. The forest floor is a mass of impenetrable bushes, vines, and tangled roots.

As suddenly as it begins, so the forest ends. As far as the eye can see, the savanna rolls gently into the distance, covered by tall grass and a few baobab trees. This is a fertile region, crossed by many rivers. As the savanna stretches northward, it becomes the dry and drought-ridden Sahel zone of the western Sudan. Beyond the Sahel lies the Sahara.

An Urban Folk

One does not usually think of Africa as a place of cities. Yet, centuries ago, on the flat plains of the western

Baobab trees dot the open grasslands of the savanna north of the forest belt. People here are farmers and raise horses, cattle, sheep, and goats. ▼

Sudan and in the forests of the Guinea coast, many cities flourished.

In the seventh century A.D., the town of Kumbi Saleh, home of the great kings of ancient Ghana, was an important marketplace. By the fifteenth century, larger towns and cities in the western Sudan, such as Timbuktu, Jenne (je ne), Gao (GAH oh), and Kano (KAHN oh), were known the world over as centers of trade and learning. Some of the cities had populations of 100,000 or more people.

There were also several important towns and cities in Guinea, including Oyo and Ibadan (Yoruba towns now located in modern Nigeria) and Kumasi (an Ashanti town located in present-day Ghana). In all of these towns and cities, the royal palace was the center of activity. Families that were related to one another lived together in compounds in special wards around the palace. Other areas were set aside for strangers.

The Yoruba towns and cities were surrounded by one or more thick, high mud walls with several gates. The walls enclosed not only family com-pounds but also plenty of farmland—often enough to feed the entire city for long periods in case of emergency. These cities were the centers of government, each ruled by its king or chief. As in the western Sudan, some of the cities became the capitals of larger states or kingdoms.

In the western Sudan, townspeople were rarely farmers. They were merchants, scholars, artisans, or slaves, who obtained their food from farmers outside the towns. In the Guinea states, however, townspeople were also farmers. A farmer may have spent much time on his land miles away from the city, but he was nevertheless a townsman, with a house and family in the city.

This urban pattern of development is rare in Africa. In the northeast and along the Mediterranean coast, first the Nile civilizations, then the Greeks, Romans, and Arabs, built great cities such as Alexandria, Cairo, Tunis, and Algiers. On the East African coast, Muslim Africans built a chain of trading cities such as Lamu and Mombasa (Kenya) and Kilwa (Tanzania). Much later the Europeans also built cities in

In the 1920s only about 5 percent of the African population lived in towns of more than 20,000 people. Today that figure is closer to 30 percent, as more and more people have been moving from the country to the cities. In some areas of Africa, cities have been established for centuries. In other areas, they are a relatively new phenomenon. In attempts to avoid the overcrowding and poverty of some modern African cities, rural people who abandoned their land are being encouraged to return to it.

Africa such as Cape Town (South Africa), Dakar (Senegal), and Nairobi (Kenya). In the rest of Africa, however, people lived in small villages or, if they were nomadic, in temporary dwellings.

From Cities to States

Most of the people of Guinea lived in the dense forests along the coast. The climate and disease must have made life very harsh. Communications were difficult, and crops were limited by the lack of sunlight. Yet, despite these drawbacks, several well-organized and sophisticated cultures developed and thrived in the heart of the forest. What were their origins? That puzzle has still not been entirely solved. But some common features of these cultures have been identified.

The western Sudan north of the Guinea states gave rise to many great kingdoms, such as Ghana, Mali (both different from the present-day nations of Ghana and Mali), and Songhay (SON gye). These kingdoms thrived on the centuries-old trade of gold and salt. But each grew to power in its turn as a result of its sophisticated form of government, which is often referred to as the "Sudanic state."

The Sudanic state centered around a strong leader or king. He either claimed descent from a god or was believed to be a god. Although the leader wielded enormous power, the government had many levels that usually ensured that this power was not abused. Nevertheless, culture revolved around the king, and larger towns and cities developed around a king's palace.

These towns often became important market centers on trade routes that stretched thousands of miles in all directions. Through taxes and tribute the kings became extraordinarily wealthy. They could afford huge armies with well-equipped cavalries. These troops helped to keep the trade routes safe and to build kingdoms by expanding the holdings and power of the city-states.

This general pattern of government and development was well established in the western Sudan by the eighth century A.D. And by the thirteenth century, the Africans of Guinea had fully adapted the system for their own use. Oduduwa—the "father" of the Yoruba people—was believed to have founded the city of Ife. His sons and grandsons, who were all leaders in their own right, founded other Yoruba cities, such as Oyo and Benin. These cities became the capitals of city-states and then of large kingdoms. Other Guinea states followed the same model.

Various other factors help to explain the rise of the western Sudanese and Guinea kingdoms. Certainly ancient Ghana (A.D. 300–1100) could not have come to power without iron weapons. These stronger, sharper, and more durable weapons gave the Ghanaians an advantage over their neighbors, who fashioned their weapons out of wood, bone, or copper. Iron farming tools also helped people to produce more crops.

The vital knowledge of ironworking traveled south to Guinea some time between A.D. 300 and 500, giving some groups there an advantage over others. At Ife, archaeologists have found traces of a settlement and iron artifacts dating to the ninth century A.D. and have formed various theories about why Ife became the first Yoruba city. Some have suggested that when

Oduduwa arrived there, he carried the knowledge of ironworking with him. Others have hypothesized that people living nearby may already have been skilled ironworkers, since there is evidence that people from Nok, which is not far from Ife, were working iron by 500 or 400 B.C.

Unlike other Yoruba cities, Ife, located at the edge of the forest, enjoyed the advantages of both the forest and the savanna. The soil there was fertile and the rainfall high. People could grow a greater variety of root and cereal crops in the savanna than was possible in the forest. They could also raise domestic animals.

The forests, however, had their own advantages. Botanists have determined that several species of yam, the kola (KOH luh) tree (which produces the valuable kola nut), and the oil palm grew centuries ago in the Guinea forests. These, along with hunted game and fish, would have provided a balanced diet. Later, European traders introduced the plantain and the banana, which originally came from Malaysia. Maize and cassava, brought from the

Vendors at a forest market sell yams, plantains, palm kernels, kola nuts, and green vegetables. Forest people also eat snails, dried fish, small deer, bush pigs, and porcupine.

Americas, also became staple forest foods. With abundant sources of food, the forest population could increase. Today some Guinea states have the highest population densities in all of Africa.

The Trade Network

With advanced iron tools and clever farming techniques, the Guinea people could produce extra food for sale. With plenty of food, a large population, and many cities, the stage was set for the development of an extensive trade network.

In fact, the market system in Guinea became larger and more complex than anywhere else in Africa. Through trade, kings and cities became wealthy, and the cities developed into larger city-states or kingdoms. As the cities grew in size and sophistication, there was a greater demand for specialized skills. The people of Guinea became experts at weaving cloth and at working metal, ivory, and wood. Only a high standard of living and a stable economy could have supported the artists who created the remarkable sculptures of Ife and Benin.

The trade network was not confined to the Guinea states alone. Forest products traveled north along well-established trade routes to the great market cities of Niani (nee AH nee), Timbuktu, and Jenne. In these places the kola nut, a mild stimulant, was much in demand. Cloth, ivory, and slaves were also trade staples. The commodity valued above all others, however, was gold.

Gold was deposited in huge quantities in the flood areas of the many great rivers flowing across West Africa. In certain areas of Guinea, people like the Wangara (wahn GAH rah), who lived south of the Senegal River, knew how to find and mine gold. They also knew the value of gold and kept the whereabouts of their mines secret.

For centuries, Berber merchants from the North African coast had crossed the Sahara by camel to trade their goods—especially salt from the desert salt mines—for the gold of Guinea. This salt-gold trade helped to create the legendary wealth of the Sudanese kings to the north, who collected heavy taxes from merchants passing through their lands. Mansa Musa, for

It is man who counts.

I call upon gold:

It answers not.

I call upon rich fabric:

It answers not.

It is man who counts.

—*Traditional Akan poem*

Gold from the West African coast was superior to that found anywhere else in the world and thus commanded higher prices than other gold. The coastal nations of West Africa were known collectively as Guinea, so the British labeled gold from the Guinea coast "Guinea gold." The English pound was usually worth 20 shillings. When backed by Guinea gold, however, it was worth 21 shillings and was known as a guinea.

example—one of the great kings of Mali—was among the richest men the world has ever known. On a visit to Cairo in 1324, he spent or gave away so much gold that the value of the metal fell dramatically and remained low for the next decade!

In many ways, gold defined the history of the Guinea states. Their gold traveled north thousands of miles across the desert to the mints and palaces of North Africa, Europe, Egypt, and Arabia. With this African gold, European nations were able to build their economies and become world powers. In the fifteenth century, it was gold that drew the Portuguese farther south along the West African coast. And in 1590 the lure of Guinea gold led the Moroccans to invade and conquer Songhay, one of the last and most powerful of the Sudanese kingdoms.

The Guinea states developed a little later than those of the western Sudan, but the two regions were closely connected. Whatever happened in one region affected the other. After Islam was brought to the western Sudan, first by Arab merchants and then by Muslim leaders, it filtered south to the Guinea states. And when the slave trade began, the havoc it caused along the Guinea coast was soon felt in the western Sudan.

The Slave Trade

Africa meant little to Europeans until the fifteenth century. In the tenth century, they were busy fighting off raids by the Muslim Arabs. Invasions by Asian nomads and later, the Vikings, followed. Between the eleventh and thirteenth centuries, Europe's energy was used up with the Crusades against the Muslim Turks in the Holy Lands. In the fourteenth century, the Black Death ravaged Europe, killing off at least two thirds of the population. Africa—all except the northern coast along the Mediterranean—was a fairy tale place, unknown and of little interest. In the last years of the fifteenth century, however, the Europeans' view of Africa was to change forever.

The Human Cargo

Until the mid-fifteenth century, trade in spices, silks, and gems from the Far East was brisk in Europe. These goods were brought overland to Europe from the Far East via Constantinople (Istanbul). In 1453 the Turks took control of the overland routes when they captured Constantinople. Once in control, they refused passage to European traders and also dramatically raised the prices of luxury goods from the Far East. Europeans had to find new routes to the East to ensure that the flow of goods from there was not interrupted. Now, however, the Far East could be reached only by sea. The Europeans raced to design ships that could travel faster and farther than ever before. The Portuguese sailing ship known as the caravel proved the winner.

The Italian explorer Christopher Columbus thought he could reach the East by sailing west. But the Portuguese thought they might reach the east by sailing around Africa to India. No one had ever sailed around the horn or tip of Africa before. In fact, the Portuguese had no idea of Africa's shape or how long their journey might take. But the lure of the great profits to be made from spices and other luxury goods from India was strong. The Portuguese had another important economic motive for sailing down the coast of West Africa. They had long known that the source of most of their gold lay somewhere south of the Sahara. If they could find it, the gold might finance the rest of their voyage around Africa and, they hoped, on to India.

The Portuguese first reached the Guinea coast near the location of

Ghana, then known as Akan, in 1471. With the permission of the Akan rulers, they built a fort called El Mina (el MEE nah) (the mine) to protect their trading post from other Europeans, who soon followed. They traded copper, brass, and other metal goods for the gold, cloth, and ivory that the Africans willingly exchanged.

When the Portuguese began their journey, trading for slaves had not been their priority. The first few slaves were taken to Europe as an exotic novelty. Soon, however, they became fashionable in upper-class circles. Slaves commanded high prices on the market, and before long, the slow trickle of slaves to Europe became a flood. By 1550, African slaves made up at least 10 percent of the population of Lisbon, Portugal's capital.

Meanwhile, the Portuguese were developing sugar plantations on islands off the central African coast that had previously been uninhabited. African slaves from the mainland

In 1482 the Portuguese built a fort on the Akan (Ghana) coast. It was Europe's first stronghold in black Africa. Because the Europeans believed that gold for which they traded was mined, they called the fort São Jorge de Mina (soun ZHOR zhe de MEE nah)—St. George of the Mine—which was shortened to El Mina. The gold was not actually mined but panned from river deposits. ▶

The word *slave* derives from the Portuguese use of Slavs, people from the Slavic nations of southern Russia, as unpaid labor on their plantations in the Mediterranean.

were used as labor on the plantations. This system was not new to the Portuguese. They already had plantations at home and on some islands in the Mediterranean, which were worked by slaves from North Africa and southern Russia. Now they simply extended their plantation system southward. After 1492, when Columbus had arrived in the Americas, the Portuguese plantation system became the model for plantation slavery in the "new world."

At first, the Portuguese themselves kidnapped Africans to sell as slaves. But they feared counterattacks from angry African people. They also realized that they alone could not hope to supply the growing demand for slaves in the Americas. In addition, they wanted to trade in other goods, such as gold, ivory, and pepper. This trade could flourish only under peaceful, stable conditions. So, instead of capturing slaves themselves, the Portuguese and other Europeans encouraged African kings and merchants, who captured huge numbers of slaves during their own wars, to become the main suppliers of the slave market.

At first most slaves came from the region that is now Senegal and Gambia, and were transported to farms in Spain or Portugal or to São Tomé (soun toh MAY), one of the islands off the Guinea coast where the Portuguese had established sugar plantations. Before long, though, slaves were being drawn from Dahomey, Oyo, Benin, and most other places along the Guinea coast. Soon the slave trade engulfed not only all of West Africa but vast areas of the rest of the continent as well.

Expansion of the Slave Trade

While the Portuguese were trading in Africa, Columbus reached the Americas. To the Europeans, the Americas were a vast "new world" with a wealth of natural resources to be exploited. By the sixteenth century, the Portuguese and Spanish had developed silver mines and highly profitable sugar, tobacco, and cotton plantations in South America and Central America.

Europe could not provide enough people to work these plantations and mines. Captured Native Americans died too easily from diseases brought

◀ Olaudah Equiano was 11 when he was captured by slave raiders near Benin in 1756. He was sold in Barbados and resold in Virginia. Equiano eventually bought his freedom and became a sailor. Known as Gustavus Vassa, he became one of the black leaders for the abolition of slavery. In 1793, Equiano's published memoirs revealed the agony of being wrenched from his home, the torture of the transatlantic crossing, and his later life in America and England. His book is an important primary source for historians of the slave trade.

by the Europeans and from the trauma of slave labor. Africans, on the other hand, fared better. Many of them had experience and skills in mining, metalworking, and tropical agriculture in their home regions. They had some immunity to tropical diseases and, because of their long contact with Europeans, to diseases spread by them. Above all, Africans were available in vast numbers.

In 1532 the first shipload of African captives crossed the Atlantic. Over the next 300 years, the transportation of captive people was developed and carried out on the largest scale ever in history.

Africa and the International Trade Network

To the European merchants involved in the slave trade, the export of

Protest and Resistance

From the start, captive Africans resisted their enslavement. There were many revolts aboard the slave ships, and on land every opportunity was taken to escape. Many captives committed suicide rather than remain slaves. In Brazil, runaway slaves set up an independent republic called Palmares. It lasted almost a hundred years before being overcome by the Portuguese. In Jamaica, escaped slaves known as Maroons set up their own farming community in the remote highlands, where their descendants still live. In 1791, slaves on the French island colony of Saint Domingue rose up and killed their white masters. They established the independent Republic of Haiti.

Africans across the Atlantic was only one part of a wider system known as the "triangular trade." Ships from Britain, Denmark, Holland, France, Spain, and Portugal brought cheap manufactured goods—mostly cloth, metal hardware, and guns—to West Africa. These were exchanged for slaves, who were transported to South America, the West Indies, and the southern colonies of the United States. From there, plantation goods such as cotton, sugar, rum, coffee, and tobacco were taken back to Europe. At each stage of the journey, European merchants made huge profits.

The great economic successes in the Americas spurred the Europeans to seek more new lands for colonies and trade goods. The seagoing nations of Europe—England, Spain, Holland, France, Italy, and Portugal—owned most of the world's great ships. With them, and their superior cannons, the Europeans were able to gain control of the world's waterways. By the mid-eighteenth century, the European powers ruled North America and South America, India, and Australia and had other colonies all over the world. They also controlled the financing of trade between these regions. They decided what was bought or sold in each place.

NORTH
AMERICA

P

The Atlantic Slave Trade

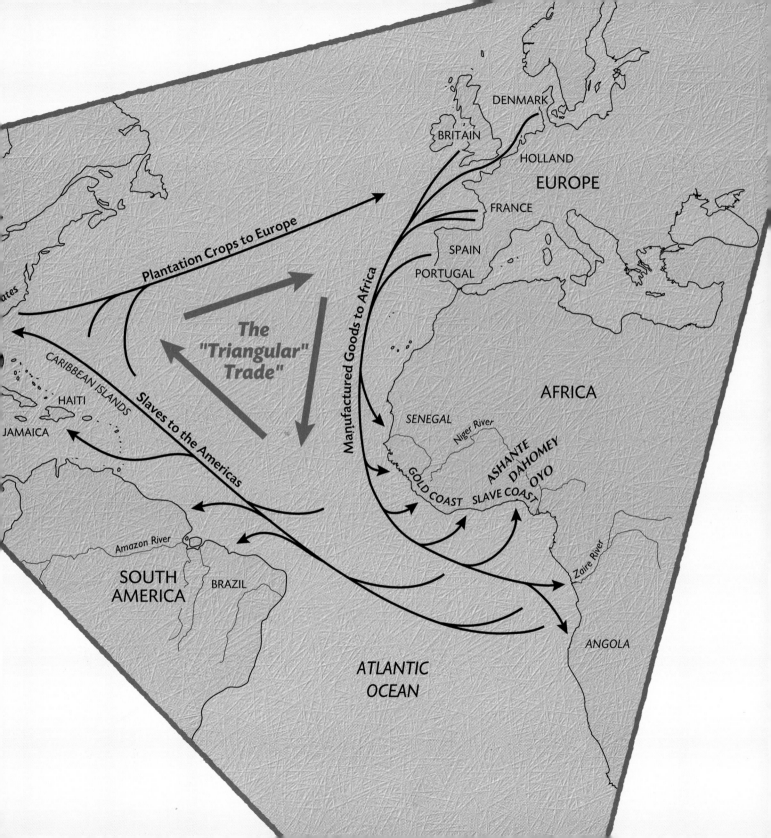

Africa quickly became entangled in a web of international trade over which it had little control. Its imports and exports were decided by the needs of Europe at any given time, not by the needs of Africans. And for 400 years the European economy needed slaves.

Africa hardly benefited from the triangular trade. At first, Africans had little idea of the market value of their raw products—ivory, ebony, leather, gold, and gum—or of slaves in the markets abroad. The goods they received in return were often poor-quality, secondhand items, such as scarves and glass beads—of hardly any use in Europe and of less use in Africa.

European merchants, however, saw large returns from the triangular trade. A single slave brought in a profit of 300 to 800 percent! Through the slave trade, European port cities like Liverpool and Bristol (England), Amsterdam (Holland), and Nance (France) prospered. In the late eighteenth century, the special manufacture of cheap guns for the African market brought huge profits to the British industrial town of Birmingham.

By 1850, one fourth of all the world's trade passed through Great Britain's ports.

These profits were reinvested in Europe, not in Africa. They helped push first Britain and then the rest of Europe into the Industrial Revolution. In Europe, new machines for agriculture and manufacturing were invented. Factories could now cheaply mass-produce goods that were exported the world over. The great increase in trade was accompanied by major developments in banking. A feudal society during the Middle Ages, Europe had now become a capitalist society, based on mass production and a system of profit and loss.

West Africa was to follow an entirely different course.

The Numbers

Historians cannot agree on the number of Africans exported in the transatlantic trade. Records show that at least 10 million captives landed alive and were sold in the Americas and the Caribbean between 1532 and the 1830s. At least 2 million captives died

on the voyage, making the total 12 million.

In the sixteenth century a few thousand slaves were transported each year. In the seventeenth century the number rose to about 20,000 annually. In the eighteenth century the number and size of plantations increased, and demand rocketed to between 50,000 and 100,000 slaves a year. One third of the slaves on the plantations died

◀ In 1807, Britain, the largest single exporter of slaves, abolished the slave trade. Denmark banned the trade in 1805, the United States in 1808, and Holland and France in 1814 and 1817, respectively. Although many Europeans and Africans had fought to end the slave trade on moral grounds, it finally ceased for economic rather than humanitarian reasons. Expansion of Caribbean sugar plantations led to a surplus, which caused prices to fall. At the same time, West African rulers were charging higher prices for their captives. Profit levels sank. Plantation owners, who had borrowed large sums of money from European banks, were unable to repay their debts. The bankers found it more profitable to invest in the new industries at home.

within three years. Few survived beyond ten years. Most died from overwork, starvation, and heartbreak. The high death rate required a continuous flow of replacements.

Some historians believe that a large amount of trade in slaves went unrecorded. The real numbers are possibly more than double those registered—perhaps 30 or 40 million. The effects of this assault on the African people were devastating.

The Aftermath

Wars had always been frequent in West Africa, and war captives had always become slaves. The high prices for captives offered by European traders undoubtedly encouraged further warfare. This was especially true in the eighteenth century, when guns primarily were traded for slaves. Soon, African rulers were caught in a vicious circle. They wanted guns to use in expanding their kingdoms, which brought them more captives to sell as slaves to get more guns. One French eyewitness to this practice noted, "Our own criminal greed has turned these people into wild animals."

The wars and the slave raids also produced many refugees. To escape the terror of war and kidnapping, many people fled their homelands, moving sometimes hundreds of miles away. In some areas, crops were abandoned and harvests neglected. Without their ancestral lands, the social structure and spiritual beliefs of many peoples were weakened.

As the slave trade wore on, more and more European ships arrived on the Atlantic coast of Africa. Soon, much of the gold, ivory, leather, and other goods that had been carried north

across the Sahara by camel was transported south and onto ships bound for the Americas and Europe. Trade along the trans-Saharan routes in the western Sudan was reduced by at least half. This loss of trade and revenue affected all the lands from Guinea to the North African coast.

At the start of European trade with West Africa, the Portuguese had brought raw materials such as copper and other metals to offer in exchange for gold. In later centuries, however, European traders brought cheaply manufactured cotton cloth, brass bowls, and other items to trade that local Africans had traditionally made themselves. Valuable African crafts, which were so closely linked to African social structure and religious beliefs, became virtually worthless next to these imported goods.

The most devastating effect of the shift in trade from goods to humans, however, was the removal of millions of West Africa's healthiest men, women, and children from their homelands. Many of these people were already slaves in Africa, but at least their work had contributed to the local economy. Now their labor would benefit masters thousands of miles away.

In addition, one report indicates that in one group of 130 captives 25 could write Arabic. It appears, then, that the captives included not only the strongest workers but also the most educated people—the very ones who might have furthered learning and supported progress in their own nations. The loss to Africa in terms of human potential was beyond measure.

Benin—A Warrior Kingdom

Oba Esigie Defeats the Idah

War came suddenly. Day and night, the drums echoed throughout the great city of Benin. In the remote areas of the forest, other drums beat out the rhythms of war, summoning men from near and far to gather at the capital. They were to march against the ruler of Idah (EE dah), a city-state several days' journey from Benin.

From every corner of the kingdom, the troops poured in. Foot soldiers and farmers, each had his oblong shield woven of palm leaves or of beaten elephant hide. Each carried his leather helmet, his spear, his bows and his arrows, and his short sword slung under his arm.

Soon the city was swarming with young men. They danced and sang all night. In the markets the armorers worked ceaselessly to hammer out swords and spearheads. Priests prepared charms to protect the soldiers or brewed the special poison for their arrows. Women sold pots of palm wine, dried fish, yams, and plantains for the soldiers to take with them.

In the deep and secret parts of the palace of King Esigie (e SEE gee ye) other preparations were made. There were sacrifices to the king's ancestors and to Ogun (oh GOON), god of iron, hunters, and war. The soothsayers threw their beads and shook their heads, trying to see the outcome of the war. And all the while, the great drums beat night and day, whipping the soldiers into a frenzy and spreading the word far and wide: King Esigie, the great *oba* of Benin, was preparing for war.

When dawn broke on the seventh day, the king was ready. The royal musicians caused a great cacophony with their booming gongs and wailing flutes. Esigie strode from his palace. He was surrounded by his bodyguards, splendid in their scarlet cloaks. The sun gleamed on their black spear blades. To a great din of shouting, whinnying horses, singing, and drums, the cavalcade moved down the long main thoroughfare of the city and out of the north gate.

Once the king had passed, the entire army followed. Hour after hour, foot soldiers tramped through the gate and disappeared into the forest. Far away to the north, distant drums and horns sounded where the king's troops led the way along the path to Idah.

It was evening before the last soldiers left Benin. At last, the city was quiet, and the huge wooden gates creaked shut. The market women packed up their goods, and the old men talked quietly in the courtyards. There was nothing to do but wait.

Along the trail to Idah, the king's troops looted houses and ransacked fields, taking whatever food they could find. As they approached the battlefront, they burned whole villages and granaries, killing anyone in their way.

One evening, as the soldiers rested, a messenger arrived. King Esigie's own mother—the queen mother—was riding at the head of her own army to support the *oba*! There was great jubilation. That night the soldiers were restless. They knew that soon the fighting would begin, and each man wondered

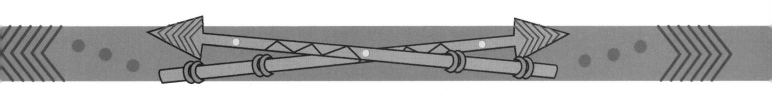

whether he would live or die. But on the very next day, they heard the far-off horns and drums of warfare long before they could reach the battlefield themselves. Before long a warrior rode into camp, his red eyes burning in his dust-covered face. Yes! There had been a battle! The queen mother's troops had ambushed the Idah army and wiped it out!

A great roar rose from the forest. King Esigie led his soldiers to the battlefield, where the fallen Idah army lay dead or dying. The sun was high, and far above, vultures circled in the sky.

The Benin soldiers moved among the bodies, collecting weapons and shields. Others ran into the forest to capture escaping Idah soldiers. Those still alive were stripped naked, roped together, and marched back to Benin. Their lives as free men were ended. From now on, they would be slaves.

That night the *oba* ordered a feast, and the two armies celebrated. The soldiers exchanged stories glorifying the heroic deeds of the queen mother and the mystical power of Oba Esigie, their great king.

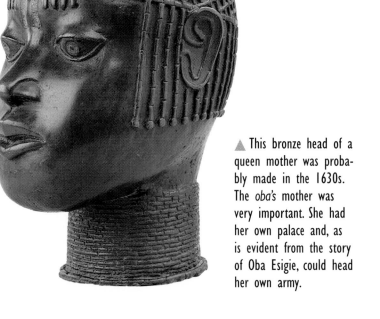

▲ This bronze head of a queen mother was probably made in the 1630s. The *oba's* mother was very important. She had her own palace and, as is evident from the story of Oba Esigie, could head her own army.

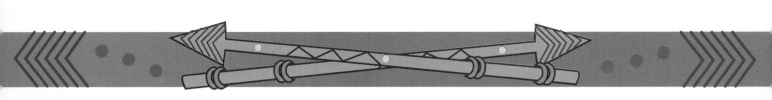

The *oba* of Benin, carrying a ceremonial hammer, is depicted on one of the great bronze plaques found in the city. The awesome power of the *oba* was described by a sixteenth-century Dutch sailor: "No one at the king's court dares to wear an item of clothing unless it has been given him by the king. . . . No one lets his hair grow unless allowed to do so by the king." No one could speak directly to the king. People's messages and requests were relayed to him by a special officer.

D'Aveiro described the great quantity of pepper to be found in Benin. The Portuguese sent samples of it all over Europe, developing a thriving market for the popular spice.

The Portuguese in Benin

In 1472, Ruy de Sequira (roi de se KEE ruh), an adventurous Portuguese sea captain, became the first European to enter the city of Benin. Benin was, and still is, located near the west bank of the Niger River, some 200 km (120 mi) north of the Niger's delta. De Sequira was greeted by Oba Ewuare (e woo AH-ray), who had ruled his kingdom sternly for more than 30 years. Ewuare had vastly increased his territory by conquering 201 towns and villages and forcing the people to pay him tribute. He had built good roads throughout his lands and encouraged ivory and wood carvers to develop their art at his palace. He had traveled far and wide to what are now the Congo region and the nation of Guinea.

At this time the kingdom of Benin was at the height of its considerable power and ruled almost one third of the Guinea coast. The Portuguese were impressed with what they saw, and they left behind various written accounts. From that point on, the history of Benin became part of European history as well.

In 1486 the Portuguese king sent João Afonso d'Aveiro (zhoun ah FON soh dah VEY roh) to Benin. Unlike de Sequira, d'Aveiro was not merely a sea captain but a nobleman sent as an ambassador from one king to another. De Sequira had received little attention from the *oba*. But d'Aveiro was remembered centuries later in the traditions of the royal court and on the bronze plaques that recorded important events in Benin's history.

D'Aveiro returned to Benin in or around 1504 to find a new *oba* in power. This was Esigie, a king determined to increase the power of Benin even further. Esigie gave d'Aveiro a royal welcome, and Portuguese soldiers went to the battlefront in the war against the Idah.

Oba Esigie wanted to encourage the Portuguese for several reasons. One was to expand trade. But the other was to get hold of Portuguese guns. Up until then, battles in the forest were conducted mostly in hand-to-hand combat. With guns Esigie could command the forest from one end to the other. He could collect many war captives, who could be sold to the

Europeans as slaves in exchange for more guns. In this way Benin, too, like many other African regions, became involved in the transatlantic slave trade.

D'Aveiro developed an interesting relationship with Oba Esigie. He advised the king to accept Christianity, which, he said, would bring his people learning, greater contact with the outside world, and salvation in God's eyes. To consider this proposal, Esigie sent a priest named Ohen-Okun (oh HEN oh KOON) as ambassador to Lisbon. Ohen-Okun was "a man of good speech and natural wisdom," wrote one chronicler. The *oba* also asked the king of Portugal to send his priests in return, that the *oba* might learn of their faith. This was done. The missionaries were successful, baptizing thousands of converts. When d'Aveiro died in Benin, he was buried with great ceremony and was much mourned by the *oba* and Christians of Benin.

Ties between Benin and Portugal became even closer as time passed. In 1553 a Portuguese trader noted that the king of Benin "could speak the Portuguese language and had learned it as a child." Many Benin merchants also learned some Portuguese. For more than 100 years, Portugal and Benin maintained friendly contact with one another.

The City and Palace
When the Portuguese arrived on the Benin coast, the king's guards escorted them through the forest to the capital. When they saw Benin, they were amazed. Here, in the heart of the deepest forest, lay a magnificent city.

The strangers stood beneath the great inner wall of the city and marveled at its size and strength. It was made of mud and was almost 10 km (6 mi) long, 9 m (30 ft) wide, and as high as a two-story house. Five thousand men had built it, piling up almost 1.5 million cubic meters (48 million cubic feet) of earth.

The Portuguese entered the city through a massive fortified gate. Armed soldiers regarded them with astonishment but allowed them to pass, and the great wooden doors swung open.

European traders marveled at the skill and organization of African traders. "These Africans," a sea captain warned, "are very wary people in their bargaining. Use them gently, for they will not traffic or bring in any wares if they are badly treated." The Africans organized boycotts and halted all trade immediately if a single item was stolen. They were tough businessmen, willing to wait ten days or longer for the right price.

Ahead of the Europeans, people thronged a wide earthen road that ran as far as the eye could see. To the left of the main highway was the city. It was larger than most European cities of the time and was divided by broad streets into special family wards. Everything was as neat as a pin. The mud houses stood close together, their walls polished to the smoothness of glass. Hidden within were sometimes 20 or more small courtyards. Hundreds of wives, children, relatives, visitors, and servants

might live under the roof of a single wealthy nobleman.

The courtyards served as bedrooms, living rooms, and dining rooms. They were surrounded by roofed galleries, one of which was always a shrine.

Seven Lice and the First King of Benin

At one time, it was said, there were no kings of Benin. But one day, the Edo people who lived in Benin were arguing about who should lead them. They could not resolve the quarrel. So they sent word to Oduduwa, the Yoruba founder and king of Ife, asking for one of his sons to rule them. But Oduduwa was wise. Why should he risk one of his sons? Instead he sent seven tiny lice to be guarded carefully and returned in three years' time. The lice were looked after in the hair of a slave, and after three years, they were fatter than before. Oduduwa was pleased. If the Edo cared so well for such lowly creatures, surely they were worthy of his son. He sent Oranmiyan to become the first *oba* of Benin. The city of Benin still exists. Its current *oba* traces his ancestry all the way back to Oduduwa.

◀ The city of Benin was drawn and described by a seventeenth-century Dutch visitor. Note the towering spires of the king's palace. "Once a year, the king appears in public, high on horseback, in all his royal regalia, followed by three or four hundred members of the court on foot and on horseback, and by a group of musicians. . . . For the king's amusement, chained and tamed leopards, several dwarfs and slaves are brought forth."

Many gods might be worshipped with statuettes or clay figurines of people or animals, and religious ceremonies were held frequently.

As they wandered about the city, always escorted by guards, the Portuguese realized that each craft occupied its own section of town. There were weavers, drum makers, leather workers, brass smiths, ivory carvers, and many other artisans. Each trade guild had its own leader.

Many of the craft workers, such as the bronze casters and wood and ivory carvers, were employed only by the *oba*. The *oba* gave permission for trade with outsiders, and the *oba* owned all the most valuable goods— ivory, slaves, leopard skins, all the pepper harvested, palm kernels, and the prized red coral that decorated his clothes. All life centered around the *oba*, and all paths led to his palace.

The Portuguese caught sight of the palace to the right of the main thoroughfare. Above its high, smooth walls, they saw steep roofs and pointed towers. At the top of each tower, a gleaming bronze eagle stared down at the city. Under armed guard the Portuguese were admitted through the gate and into the inner courtyards.

The palace itself was as big as a small city. There were three separate sections. In one part lived the officials and slaves (together with all their wives and children) who looked after the *oba*'s clothes, ornaments, and ceremonial regalia. Those who cared for the *oba's* wives and children had another section to themselves. In the third part lived the *oba* himself, surrounded by hundreds of personal servants.

Everywhere there were shrines, each dedicated in some way to the *oba*. Some shrines were to his ancestors, some to different parts of his body. There were hundreds of bronze and ivory heads and figurines. Sacred bells and clappers, used to summon the spirits, lay on shelves along with carvings of the sacred leopard. Huge elephant tusks, intricately carved from end to end, were propped against the walls.

At last the Portuguese entered the central chambers of the palace, where the *oba* lived. From outside, they had seen the eagles atop the 18-meter (60-foot) towers. Now inside, they saw a giant copper snake curved downward from the peak of the central tower almost to the floor. On walls and pillars were the incredible bronze plaques on which the history of Benin had been commemorated forever. From then on, these plaques would also include images of the Portuguese—hunting, trading, and fighting alongside their African hosts.

The Fall of Benin

The Portuguese had seen Benin at the height of its power. Profits from the slave trade, along with the muskets and cannon sold by the Europeans, allowed the *obas* of Benin to expand their kingdom ever outward. Their

Portuguese soldiers similar to this one appear on the Benin plaques. The plaques depict life in the kingdom over several centuries. The plaques helped court historians recall events of the past. ▶

armies were constantly on the warpath, eager to capture more and more slaves. In the city of Benin, the power of the *obas* and the splendor of the palace became greater than ever before.

By the beginning of the eighteenth century, however, the kingdom had sadly deteriorated. Two hundred years of constant war had taken a toll on the land and people. Slave raids had ravaged huge areas of the country. The survivors had fled, letting the forest overgrow their farmland. The African slavers found it increasingly difficult to find victims from other areas and began to fight one another. Even in the city of Benin, citizens were captured and sold. The entire kingdom was severely weakened through these internal struggles.

Slaves, pepper, ivory, gum, and cotton cloth had been the mainstays of trade with the Europeans. As the supply of all these commodities steadily dwindled, the Europeans found little reason to trade with Benin. The financial basis of the kingdom collapsed. Meanwhile, the British, who had followed the Portuguese in establishing trading posts along the Guinea coast, had become deeply involved in the affairs of Benin. They wanted total control of trade along the Niger River. The city of Benin was the last stronghold in their way, and they were determined to destroy it. In 1897, nine Europeans were killed in Benin. Immediately the British saw their chance to retaliate. Twelve hundred British soldiers marched into the city, where they froze in horror at what they saw:

"Blood was everywhere. . . . On the right was a crucifixion tree with a double crucifixion on it, the two poor wretches stretched out facing west, with their arms bound together in the middle. . . . At the base were skulls and bones . . . the debris of former sacrifices, and down every main road were two or three more human sacrifices."

This report appeared in the *Spectator*, a British newspaper, on January 16, 1897. The headline was "Benin—City of Blood"—a label that the British deliberately used to justify their questionable actions in Benin and that unfortunately clings to the city to this day. However, the British had completely failed to understand what they had found in Benin.

Before the British invasion the kingdom of Benin had been devastated by internal problems. Then its people and even its kings had watched with horror as one powerful kingdom in the region after another fell to the British. The people of Benin had invested their last hopes in their *oba*. They were certain that his awesome power and his magic would save them.

Human sacrifice was not then—nor has it ever been—a common African custom. But in Benin, as the British advanced ever closer, the people's despair was overwhelming. The priests believed that they had somehow angered their great spirit. To appease him they gave up more and more human lives. But it was too late. The power of the *oba* and his kingdom was broken forever. Only the great Benin bronzes, the ivory and terracotta masks and figurines—the art of great African masters—remain today as a testament to the kingdom's former glory.

▲ As Oba Esigie marched to fight the Idah in 1515, he heard the ominous sounds of a hornbill or ibis overhead. This was an evil omen. Oba Esigie ordered the bird to be killed, and then went on to defeat the Idah in battle. From then on, bronze images of the bird were flogged at court ceremonies to remind the bird that the *oba* was above the fate of ordinary mortals.

Ashanti— People of the Forest
Osei Tutu Receives the Golden Stool

In the village the drummers beat out their message to all who could hear and understand: "Akwome (ah KWOH me) the storyteller is coming! Akwome is coming!"

From miles around, people gathered in the village. Everyone was excited, for Akwome was a master teller of tales. In one story she aroused laughter over the escapades of Ananse (ah NAHN se) the Spider. In another, Akwome reminded her listeners that Nyankopon (nee AHN koh pon), the sky god, had created the mighty trees, the flowing rivers, and the very earth upon which they sat, and they gazed in awe at the towering canopy of the forest.

When everyone was gathered under the tree, and the gentle light of evening flooded the clearing, Akwome began.

"Let the drums be silent!" she commanded. "Draw near and listen, my people. And you, Sasabonsam (sah sah BON sahm), O king of evil spirits, call off your dark hordes! Let them not blame me for what I am about to tell, for I tell only what I know and what others have told me."

The listeners were silent, eager for the story to begin.

"Long, long ago," Akwome began, "there were seven Ashanti kingdoms, each ruled by a different king. Always, these kings were at war with one another, and the stronger ones overcame the weakest.

"The king of Kumasi (koo MAH see) was defeated by the king of Denkera (DEN ke rah). Now this king of Denkera was cunning. To keep his power over the people of Kumasi, he took with him the young prince called Osei (OH say) Tutu, who was next in line to the throne of Kumasi. 'If you are not obedient to my laws,' the king of Denkera threatened his new captives, 'I will kill Osei Tutu.'

"So Osei Tutu lived among the people of Denkera. But he never gave up his dream of returning one day to claim his rightful place on the throne of Kumasi.

"As he grew up, Osei Tutu heard many stories of a famous priest and magician named Okomfo Anokye (oh KOM foh ah NOHK ye).*

"Okomfo Anokye could make wonderful magic, it was said. He placed together in a box the hair from the head of a gorilla, the sharp nails of a leopard claw, and the leaves from a gardenia bush. Around this strong medicine, he danced and prayed. And when the land suffered from drought, Anokye could make rain fall from the sky. When people brought him their sick children, he could heal them. With his magic, Anokye could cause a man to die in great pain, if he so wished."

The storyteller Akwome paused. For a moment, there was silence. The children's eyes widened in awe as they thought of Okomfo Anokye, the great magician. He was the hero of the Ashanti people, and many were the stories about him that were told in the forest villages.

*Okomfo Anokye means "priest, magician, prophet."

Akwome continued.

"Osei Tutu decided to escape from the Denkera. He would find this great magician and seek his help. And that is exactly what Osei Tutu did. Early one morning, when the mists still hid the forest, he ran off. No one followed. Osei Tutu wandered for many days. Everywhere, he heard tales of the great magician, who had been traveling throughout the country to gather his wisdom. But where was he? No one knew.

"An evening came when Osei Tutu rested on the outskirts of a city. There, tied to a log, was an old man who was being punished for some mischief he had done. Osei Tutu felt sorry for him and set him free. Who could it have been, O respected listeners?"

With one voice, the villagers shouted "Okomfo Anokye!"

And they were right.

"The two decided to travel together," Akwome continued. "And in time, the news spread that the reigning king of Kumasi had died. At once, Osei Tutu and Okomfo Anokye returned to that city, and with much splendor, Osei Tutu was crowned its rightful king. He was the fourth of the Kumasi kings, and he ruled wisely and was loved by his people.

"Then there came a day when Okomfo Anokye announced that the time had come for the Ashanti people to cease their warring against each other and unite. The seven kings were called to a meeting under the great tree in Kumasi, and each king was ordered to bring his sacred stool—a symbol of respect for his ancestors. At this gathering, so it was said, Okomfo Anokye would appoint the new lord of all the Ashanti kingdoms.

"The great drums beat out the message. From the seven kingdoms, the kings arrived in Kumasi, each with his sacred stool. They sat on their thrones in the clearing, each dressed in colorful *kente* (KEN tay) cloth, shaded by a magnificent silk umbrella of many hues.

"The sacred stools were placed together in the clearing. Many, many people had gathered to see how Okomfo Anokye would appoint the new lord. As the drums whipped up a frenzied rhythm, the people became silent. For Okomfo Anokye had begun his magic.

"He placed his box of medicine in the center of the circle. He danced and prayed to the great sky god, Nyankopon. The people waited, breathless. Okomfo Anokye danced faster and faster until suddenly—behold!—a dazzling flame

Ashanti weavers produce colorful, intricately woven cloth known as *kente*. Each part of the loom has symbolic meaning. Today, *kente* is the national dress of Ghana and is worn at all important family and government occasions. Certain patterns of *kente* cloth may be worn only by royalty and chiefs. ▶

descended from the sky. One by one, the sacred stools caught fire, causing a cloud of black smoke to cover the area. Again Okomfo Anokye prayed to Nyankopon, and the people heard a mighty rumbling in the sky. Nyankopon had spoken!

"And behold, O listeners, for out of the sky came floating toward the earth a black stool. And lightly, gently, silently, it came to rest upon the knees of Osei Tutu. And as the people watched, the black stool turned to gold and shone in the sun.

"Now the people rose up and shouted with joy and Okomfo Anokye spoke to them. 'The Ashanti people will unite!' he commanded. 'No longer shall king fight king. You will join in one great kingdom, and your lord shall be Osei Tutu, for so it has been ordained.'

"Okomfo Anokye told the people the meaning of the golden stool. 'The spirit of the Ashanti dwells inside the golden stool,' he said. 'The stool represents the Ashanti people. No Ashanti king must ever oppress his people. Therefore, no one must ever sit on the golden stool.'"

Akwome paused. Then she said, "And so it has been, my people, from that day to this."

The elderly members of Akwome's audience nodded their heads in agreement. Indeed, they confirmed, since that day no one had ever sat on the sacred golden stool of the Ashanti people.

Akwome raised her hand for silence. "That is my story, my people. Whether it be sweet to your ears or not, take some with you and let some return to me. For that is my story, as I tell it to you, and as it was told to me."

And with that, Akwome the storyteller disappeared into the forest to tell her tales wherever people would listen.

Gold—Backbone of the Kingdom

Okomfo Anokye influenced Osei Tutu and the fate of the Ashanti people enormously. You may or may not believe the legend of the golden stool. But the fact remains that the stool exists and is honored to this day, and that—with the magician Anokye's help—Osei Tutu founded the Ashanti kingdom sometime during the 1670s.

Osei Tutu's kingdom was bordered on the east and north by the Volta River. Its boundary on the west was roughly the same as the boundary between present-day Ghana and Ivory Coast. The Pra River formed its southeastern border. Kumasi, the capital of the kingdom, lay just south of the kingdom's center.

The stage had been set for Osei Tutu many centuries earlier. In the fourteenth century the empire of Mali reached the height of its power. Mali was located in the grassy savanna to the north of present-day Ghana, and its great cities of Timbuktu, Gao, and Jenne were known far and wide as centers of trade and learning.

From Mali, professional traders of the Malinke (mah LIHN ke), Bambara, and Soninke (soh NIHN ke) peoples fanned out, searching for new trading opportunities. They were known in the west as the Wangara and in the east as the Dyula (dee OO luh).

These merchants, who were usually practicing Muslims, carried the trade of the Malian empire to the farthest corners of West Africa. For years, the Akan people of the forest edge had supplied traders with small quantities of gold and kola nuts. But under the influence of the Dyula, the Akan began to exploit their resources more fully. They employed slaves supplied by the Dyula to clear forest areas for farming and to mine gold. The Dyula traded the gold at the great markets of the western Sudan. From there, Arab merchants took it across the Sahara to markets in North Africa and Europe.

Eventually the Akan settled in the forest. In time, those who controlled the gold mines (perhaps because they had more slaves than others) founded small chiefdoms.

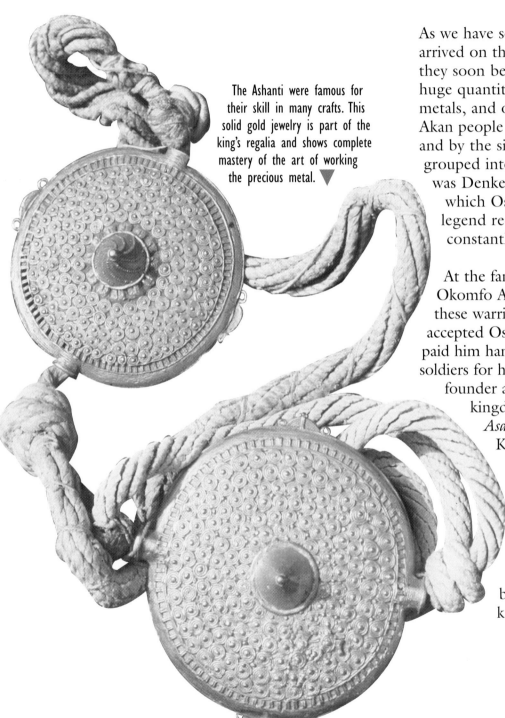

The Ashanti were famous for their skill in many crafts. This solid gold jewelry is part of the king's regalia and shows complete mastery of the art of working the precious metal. ▼

As we have seen, when the Portuguese arrived on the Akan coast in the 1470s, they soon began buying Akan gold in huge quantities, exchanging cotton cloth, metals, and other goods for the gold. The Akan people prospered from this trade, and by the sixteenth century they had grouped into several states. One of these was Denkera. Another was Kumasi, of which Osei Tutu became king. As the legend recalls, these rival states were constantly at war with one another.

At the famous meeting called by Okomfo Anokye in Kumasi, the heads of these warring states agreed to unite and accepted Osei Tutu as their overlord. They paid him handsome tribute and provided soldiers for his army. Osei Tutu, the founder and first king of the Ashanti kingdom, took on the title *Asantehene* (ah SAHN te HAY ne), King of All the Ashanti.

Osei Tutu's successor was Opoku Ware (oh POH koo WAH ray), who reigned from 1720 to 1750. Through relentless warfare, Opoku Ware expanded the boundaries of the Ashanti kingdom until it covered most

Rules of Behavior for the *Asantehene*

The successor to the throne was selected from the members of a royal clan by the reigning king's sister. She consulted with many advisors to make her choice. At the crowning of an Ashanti king, a herald would announce what was expected of the ruler.

- He should never disclose the origin of any person.
- He must never abuse anyone.
- He must never use personal violence.
- He must not call people fools.
- He must not be greedy.
- He should always be willing to listen.
- He should never act without consulting others.
- He must walk slowly and with dignity, as befits a great ruler.

The *asantehene* would reply as follows:

"If I do not rule the people well, as my forefathers and you ruled them, and if I do not listen to the advice of the councilors, then I have broken my oath and may be punished."

The punishment was death by beheading.

The Ashanti culture is matrilineal—that is, descent is counted through the mother's clan. Thus the head of the royal clan is the queen mother. Osei Tutu's mother, the queen mother, was also his advisor. She attended all councils, sitting on her son's left. As long as her clan remained in power, she retained her title.

Although a man reared and loved his own children, his greater responsibility was to his nephews and nieces— the children of his sister. They would ensure that a clan did not die out. Nephews—not sons—inherited a man's property.

---

of what is Ghana today, from the northern savanna to the coastal forest, and included parts of what are now Ivory Coast and Togo.

Asantehene Osei Kwadwo (KWAH-dwoh) (1764–1777) introduced a new, centralized form of government. He appointed government officers and military leaders on the basis of merit rather than birthright and did away with the old hereditary chiefdoms. By the time the European powers had determined to colonize West Africa in the nineteenth century, the Ashanti federation had become the most powerful and effectively run kingdom on the continent.

The Golden Stool

To the Ashanti, the golden stool which "descended from the sky" was a gift from the gods. It represented the mutual agreement between rival states to accept the authority of a single king. In other words, the stool symbolized a move away from tribalism and toward true nationhood. It may also have represented the gold, so plentiful in the kingdom, and the gold trade which later became central to the political system of the Ashanti federation. If the stool were ever to be removed or destroyed, the Ashanti believed that their culture would cease to exist.

As decreed by Okomfo Anokye, no one has ever actually sat on the golden stool. When a king is crowned, he pretends to sit on the stool, bending his knees three times while supported by attendants. During ceremonies the golden stool is carried by its own attendants under its own huge umbrella.

In the past the golden stool was always carried into battle, for not to do so would have meant defeat. At crucial moments in the fight, the chiefs and military commanders surrounded the stool. They would have set themselves

◀ The Ashanti worship stools on which important ancestors have sat. These are kept in special stool houses in each chief's household. Every 43 days, Ashanti everywhere observe a two-day festival called *adae* (ah DAY) during which they worship their ancestor's stools and thus honor the ancestors themselves.

and the stool on fire rather than let an enemy take possession of it.

In 1895, after many wars among rival Ashanti states, the British ordered a stop to the fighting so that peaceful trade might continue. They were surprised when King Prempeh, sixteenth ruler of the Ashanti, gave in without a fight. Rather than lose their golden stool in battle against British firearms, the Ashanti nation preferred to become a British protectorate.

In 1900 a British governor visiting Kumasi demanded to sit on the golden stool. The Ashanti were so enraged that they hid the stool and declared war. The stool was found 21 years later by workers digging up a road, and to this day it is safe in the hands of the Ashanti nation.

Panning, Mining, Trading

Before the Europeans arrived, gold was valued among the Ashanti for ornamental use, while cowrie shells were the most common currency. The wealth of a household—especially of a chief or member of a royal family—was displayed in magnificent gold jewelry, masks, breast-plates, headbands, knee and ankle ornaments, canes, fly whisks, and other objects of lasting beauty.

The Ashanti obtained gold by panning the sand from the riverbeds. Tiny flakes of gold, and sometimes large nuggets, were deposited there by water that had flowed over gold-bearing rocks. Later, when European demand for gold exceeded supplies, the Ashanti put their slaves to work in mines. Shafts were dug deep into the ground, and slave miners were lowered and raised on ropes, often spending days sleeping, eating, and digging in the shafts. While some gold was used for trade, a portion went to each of the chiefs and subchiefs of the area, who paid a further portion to the *asantehene.*

The Ashanti were not fools. They kept the location of their gold mines secret from the Europeans until a Frenchman named Pierre Bonnat (pee AIR boh-NAH) persuaded the *asantehene* that greater profits could be made by selling the mines to the Europeans. After that, the mining industry developed rapidly. By 1882, six European mining companies had holdings in the Ashanti

The Ashanti weighed gold dust or nuggets with gold figures of animals or symbolic designs. Some weights illustrated proverbs. One weight shows two men lying on a board, one on his back, the other on his stomach. The proverb: If I cannot see the sky god lying on my back, how can you expect to see him lying on your stomach? What might this proverb mean?

gold mines. And by 1912, roads and railways had been built to transport the gold from the mines to ships waiting at the coast.

So much gold was exported from the Guinea coast that it came to be known as the Gold Coast (later renamed Ghana). It has been estimated that between 1473 and 1903, some 65 million dollars' worth of gold was traded. Since then, with modern mining machinery, some 30 million dollars' worth of gold is exported from Ghana annually.

The Fall of Ashanti

For the first 400 years of trading on the Akan coast, Europeans lived in fear and ignorance of the rich interior lands. They had to bow to the rules made by African chiefs, who made it very clear that the Europeans were not on their own soil.

First the Portuguese, then the English, the Dutch, the Swedes, and the Danes

were permitted to build trading forts along the Akan coast. But they rarely, if ever, saw the Ashanti, for these proud people shunned outsiders. The Ashanti chiefs used traders from other tribes to bring Ashanti goods to the Gold Coast and return with European goods.

The Ashanti were wealthy enough to pay for luxuries such as cotton, silk, woolen goods, hatchets and knives, beads, iron, tobacco and tobacco pipes, guns and gunpowder, and brass bowls. In return, the Ashanti traded gold, elephants' tusks, skins, valuable timber, wax, palm oil, and slaves.

As was the case in other Guinea states, it was the traffic in slaves that helped the Ashanti become powerful. Around 1700, they began to receive firearms from the Europeans and with these were soon able to conquer most of the Gold Coast. As a result of their conquests they had many captives and became the chief suppliers of slaves to the Europeans. The Ashanti were known and feared as cunning warriors who practiced sophisticated forms of guerrilla warfare and rarely lost a battle.

In the early nineteenth century, however, Europeans raised their voices in protest against the slave trade, and it was finally banned. To enforce the ban, Britain, the strongest naval power in the world, sent a huge fleet of ships to monitor trade in the Gulf of Guinea. By the mid-nineteenth century, Britain had stopped most of the slave trade. It also claimed most of the Gold Coast's legitimate trade in palm oil, timber, diamonds, and other goods.

To the Ashanti chiefs in the interior, these changes were deeply puzzling. Why was it now *wrong* to trade in slaves when it had been right for centuries? The Ashanti had no intention of giving up a way of life that had brought them vast territories and great wealth, and so they continued their conquests and slave raids. They also skillfully played one European power against another in the competition for gold and slaves.

In 1827, the Ashanti laid siege to a British fort. There were heavy losses on both sides, and the skirmishes between the Ashanti and the British continued. Twenty-one years later, the Ashanti were "defeated" by the British and coastal tribes, who had joined forces. But the Ashanti refused to give up. In their view the British had no business interfering in their affairs! The warfare continued.

Finally, in 1873, the British governor issued the *asantehene* an ultimatum: The Ashanti must hand over all prisoners taken in battle, give up all claims over the coastal tribes they had previously conquered, remain in their forest territory, and pay 50,000 ounces of gold for past misdeeds. All this, or the British would invade Kumasi.

The Ashanti rejected the ultimatum, and the British declared war. Within two months, the British, with their superior guns and an army of 6,000 men, had defeated the Ashanti. Kumasi and much of the Ashanti kingdom were captured, and their king was sent into exile (though allowed to return later). On January 1, 1902, the British announced their rule over what we now know as Ghana. The Ashanti forest was included in the crown colony of the Gold Coast, and the northern grasslands became a protectorate. It was a sad end to this period in the history of the Ashanti people.

Epilogue

Although the slave trade was officially abolished in the early nineteenth century, illegal trading continued as long as there was a need for slaves on the American plantations. The institution of slavery itself was not abolished until 1834 in the British colonies, 1848 in the French colonies, 1865 in the southern United States, and 1888 in Brazil. Between 1807 and 1888, it is estimated that more than 1 million Africans were carried across the Atlantic.

At first the British had been the most ruthless of slave traders. They exported more African captives than any other European nation. After abolition, however, they became as intense in their efforts to stop the slave trade. Armed British ships patroled West African waters in search of illegal slave ships. And British soldiers fought on land to stop the slave caravans.

Why were the British so interested in ending slavery and establishing their presence in the lands they called Nigeria and the Gold Coast?

Despite the incessant wars and the destructive effects of the slave trade, there had been some positive developments in West Africa. African farmers had begun to grow imported American crops, such as maize and cassava. Trade in other important goods, such as ivory, gold, and rare woods, had continued along the age-old routes across the Sahara to North Africa and was further developed with the Europeans. As the trade in people ground to a halt, it was replaced by trade in non-human but highly profitable commodities, known as the "legitimate" trade.

African leaders and merchants worked to develop their trade goods. Gum arabic, a resin used to fix dyes in printed cloth, was exported from Senegal. Guinea exported groundnuts. In the Gold Coast, the Ashanti kingdom had completed its period of expansion. It had no war captives to sell, so it renewed its trade in gold. Palm oil was the major lubricant for machines abroad, as well as a primary ingredient of soap. It became the major export of the entire Guinea coast. And increasingly, trade took place

In 1879 a young blacksmith named Tete Quarshi (te te KWAHR shee) planted some cacao seeds from the island of Fernando Po, off Africa's west coast, on his farm at the Gold Coast. Five years later they bore fruit. Quarshi had started the crop that would eventually become the mainstay of Ghana's economy: cacao, which is used to make cocoa and chocolate. Today, Ghana is the world's foremost supplier of cacao. Most of it is produced by the Ashanti in the forest regions. ▶

through the exchange of money, rather than through barter.

The British wanted to command as much of the trade in West Africa as possible. They stationed their soldiers on land to "keep the peace," but their real intent was to enforce their trading rights over those of the Africans. In the 1850s the antimalarial drug quinine was discovered. The British could now live much healthier lives in West Africa. By 1864, 21 British firms had established trading posts on the Niger delta. It was not long before the British ventured even farther up the river. Their aim was to get rid of the African middlemen who supplied them with trade goods. They wanted to deal directly with merchants in the interior.

The British used brute physical force when they took over the lands of the Yoruba, Bini, and Ashanti. These nations had known war before. It was a part of life in the region. Each kingdom had been built and sustained through war, and each had felt itself justified in waging war against its neighbors.

As a result of these conflicts, boundaries had changed somewhat, and ordinary people suddenly found themselves captives of a new and foreign ruler. Certainly, people were oppressed as subjects of a foreign king. Nevertheless, their labor and their skills contributed to the regional African economy. They lived lives that were familiar to them, and they were able to understand the politics and economics of their status.

But when the British took over, Africans were faced with an entirely new way of life. The British, like all other colonial powers, felt fully justified in conquering territories in Africa. It was, in their minds, their "proper duty" to bring democracy, capitalism, and Christianity to these "poor savages." But now their African subjects worked for foreign "overlords." Their labor fueled the European, not the African, economy.

This ad promoting trade goods from British colonies in West Africa appeared in the *London Times* of December 1926. The illustration shows the "talking drums" of the Ashanti. With no written language, the Ashanti drummers passed news and messages over great distances at amazing speed, faster even than the telegraph, according to early British reports. "Male" and "female" drums produced low and high tones respectively. Drummers did not spell out single words. They used simplified sound phrases that all Ashanti could understand. ▶

NEWS FOR *YOU* FROM
WEST AFRICA

Have you ever realised that the four Colonies of British West Africa—Nigeria, the Gold Coast, Sierra Leone and Gambia are actually helping to run your home and to feed your family!

The sheets you sleep in may be woven of Nigerian cotton; the soap they are washed with is probably made of West African oils. The Gold Coast is the native land of most of the cocoa you drink and the chocolates you eat. Your grocer sells margarine made from West African nuts. Your butcher supplies beef fattened on West African oil-cake. Ginger beer and ginger cakes are made with Sierra Leone ginger. Ground nuts come from Gambia and Nigeria.

Britain has given West Africa great gifts – the end of slavery and tribal war – a new era of peace, happiness and prosperity for 23 million people spread over an area ten times the size of England.

And West Africa is rapidly becoming one of the great buyers of British manufactures. Many thousands of our people already depend for their work and wages on the ever-increasing orders which these British Colonies send us year by year.

There you see again how Empire trade benefits both the producer Overseas and your own people at Home.

* * *

The illustration is of the talking-drums with which West African natives communicate at great distances by tapping out messages.

The MESSAGE to you is
BUY EMPIRE GOODS

ISSUED BY THE EMPIRE MARKETING BOARD.

And the new religion introduced by the Europeans undermined their traditional belief systems.

The British found no reason to settle in West Africa. The region had none of the lush, well-watered lands that made parts of East and South Africa so attractive to European farmers. Instead, the Gold Coast and Nigeria became "administrative colonies," run by white governors and officials who enlisted the aid of local African leaders.

The Gold Coast was to be the showcase of the British empire in Africa. The British vastly increased the export of cocoa, gold, and timber. By the outbreak of World War I in 1914, the Gold Coast was the most prosperous colony in Africa. It became the world's leading producer of manganese and also exported diamonds and bauxite. The colony was reputed to have the best schools in Africa, a thriving free press, and an excellent civil service.

The picture was not as rosy in Nigeria. After gaining control of the region in 1902, the British took over a valuable tin-bearing zone in the central plateau area. For years, Africans had mined tin here. Now, more than 50 foreign companies controlled the mines. By 1928 they employed more than 40,000 miners. The foreign companies effectively destroyed the business of thousands of independent tin producers. They now became wage earners, as they had no other means of making a living.

Nigerian farmers fared just as badly. The British forced them to grow more cash crops, like cotton and cocoa, for export. Food crops were neglected. By 1947, there was not enough food to go around. Malnutrition was rampant. For the first time in its long history, Nigeria had to import food.

In addition, the British imposed their own arbitrary boundaries on the African nations they conquered. The Yoruba, Bini, Hausa, Igbo and many other peoples were included in the nation of Nigeria. Having been independent rivals for centuries, they were now supposed to be united as one nation and to call themselves "Nigerians." Similarly, the Ashanti and their neighbors, the Ga, the Ewe (AY way) and others, now all belonged to the Gold Coast.

Kumasi was the capital of the Ashanti kingom. It is still a thriving market city. ▶

The British administered their colonies by a system of "indirect rule." They delegated authority to village chiefs, who reported to the British government. In some areas, however, as in the Igbo territory of southeastern Nigeria, people lived simply in small family homesteads. Because there were no chiefs, the British appointed certain individuals to chiefdom. These "false" chiefs were hated by their people.

In all areas, Muslim, Christian, and traditional beliefs came into conflict more than ever before. Tensions and age-old rivalries flared.

During the 1950s the cry for independence rang throughout the African colonies. In 1957, under the leadership of Kwame Nkrumah (KWAH may en KROO mah), a young African who had studied in the United States and Great Britain, the Gold Coast became the first African nation to gain independence. Africans everywhere rejoiced. Nkrumah named the new nation Ghana in honor of ancient Ghana, the first great West African kingdom, which had risen to power in the eighth century in the area that is today Mali and Mauritania.

Nigeria won independence from Britain in 1960. Soon after, the country exploded as rival ethnic groups battled for power in the central government. One military revolt followed another, and in the civil war of 1967 at least a million people died.

Meanwhile, during the 1960s, oil was discovered beneath the Niger delta. Between 1965 and 1973, world oil prices skyrocketed. Nigeria found that it had a 5-billion-dollar surplus in its budget! The government went on a spending spree, starting up huge industrial projects. But in 1981 a worldwide recession sent oil prices plummeting, and development in Nigeria almost came to a standstill.

Today both Ghana and Nigeria suffer from many problems that are a direct result of the slave trade, British colonization, and corrupt African leadership. Both nations have also suffered from the well-meaning attempts of developed nations to guide or force "development" in West Africa.

In the south, for example, cacao trees thrive best in the shade of the forest. But attempts to increase cacao and

▲ The slave trade brought Africans from the Guinea coast to the Americas, Cuba, Haiti, Jamaica, and other Caribbean islands—collectively known as the African diaspora (dye AS por uh), or area of dispersal. The transplanted Africans kept much of their culture alive. Here, actors and actresses from the diaspora perform a play about Shango. In the foreground, Shango, with his double-headed battle ax, fights Ogun, the god of iron and war. In the background hovers the menacing death figure of Iku.

In 1986, Wole Soyinka (WOH le soi YIHN kah), a Yoruba playwright, was awarded the Nobel Prize in literature. He has written more than 20 plays, several volumes of poetry, and 2 novels. The plays combine African dance, mime, and music with western drama and often deal with a common African topic—the boundary between life and death. Soyinka's plays, which are highly critical of the Nigerian government, have been performed all over the world.

timber production have led to more forest clearing. As a result, the savanna has taken over the cleared land and cacao production has decreased.

Efforts to improve the water supply in Ghana allow people to keep larger herds of cattle, sheep, and goats. But the huge numbers of animals graze the land bare of grass and shrubs. With low rainfall and constant grazing, plants cannot grow again. Soil turns to dust. Animals, and then people, starve.

At the same time, better health care and resistance to family planning has led to a dramatic population explosion in both nations. Nigeria takes up 15 percent of the area of West Africa but has 56 percent of its population—that is, 121 million people! Before long, the people of Nigeria will need double the food that the country can supply.

If the future looks bleak, there are signs of improvement. During the 1980s, under strong leadership, Ghana's economy experienced greater growth than that of any other African nation. Nigeria still prospers from its exports of oil, coal, gold, iron ore, and other minerals. Despite yet another military coup in 1994, efforts have been made to improve education and agricultural practices.

Now that the Guinea states have entered the industrial world of the West, their "progress" is measured in terms of an individual's income in cash, or the "gross domestic product" of a nation. Western culture has truly had a deep and lasting influence on Ghana and Nigeria. Nevertheless, the Yoruba, the Bini, and the Ashanti (along with most other ethnic groups there) are still proudly distinct peoples, with their own languages, traditions, and belief systems. As long as they can remain so, perhaps this, too, should be considered a measure of progress.

Pronunciation Key

Some words in this book may be new to you or difficult to pronounce. Those words have been spelled phonetically in parentheses. The syllable that receives stress in a word is shown in small capital letters. The following pronunciation key shows how letters are used to show different sounds.

a	after	(AF tur)	oh	flow	(floh)	ch	chicken	(CHIHK un)
ah	father	(FAH thur)	oi	boy	(boi)	g	game	(gaym)
ai	care	(kair)	oo	rule	(rool)	ing	coming	(KUM ing)
aw	dog	(dawg)	or	horse	(hors)	j	job	(jahb)
ay	paper	(PAY pur)				k	came	(kaym)
			ou	cow	(kou)	ng	long	(lawng)
e	letter	(LET ur)	yoo	few	(fyoo)	s	city	(SIH tee)
ee	eat	(eet)	u	taken	(TAY kun)	sh	ship	(shihp)
				matter	(MAT ur)	th	thin	(thihn)
ih	trip	(trihp)	uh	ago	(uh goh)	thh	feather	(FETHH ur)
eye	idea	(eye DEE uh)				y	yard	(yahrd)
y	hide	(hyd)				z	size	(syz)
ye	lie	(lye)				zh	division	(duh VIHZH un)

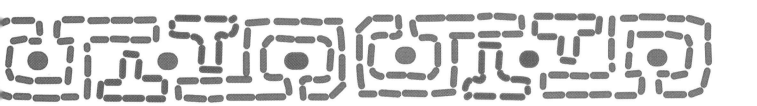

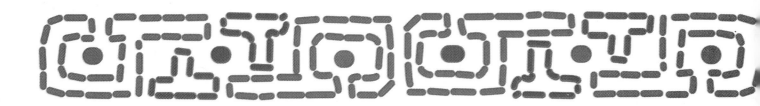

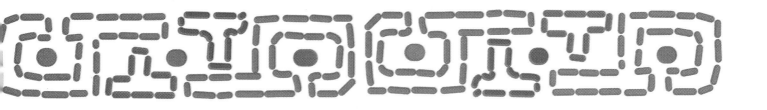

For Further Reading

(* = recommended for younger readers)

Aboyami, Fuja. *Fourteen Hundred Cowries: Traditional Stories of the Yoruba*. London: Oxford University Press, 1962.

Barker, Carol. *Kayode and His Village in Nigeria*. Oxford: Oxford University Press, 1982.*

Bleeker, S. *The Ashanti of Ghana*. New York: William Morrow, 1966.*

Boyd, Herb. *African History for Beginners*. New York: Writers and Readers Publishing, 1991.*

Brooks, Lester. *Great Civilizations of Ancient Africa*. New York: Four Winds Press, 1971.

Courlander, H. *The Hat-Shaking Dance and Other Tales From the Gold Coast.* E. M. Hale & Co., 1962.*

———. *Tales of Yoruba Gods and Heroes.* New York: Crown Publishers Inc., 1973.*

Danford, J. A. *Our Folk Lore and Fables.* Lagos: Public Relations Department, 1952.

Davidson, Basil. *Africa in History.* New York: Macmillan, 1991.

———. *African Kingdoms.* New York: Time-Life Books, 1966.

———. *A Guide To African History.* New York: Doubleday, Zenith Books, 1965.

———. *The Lost Cities of Africa.* Boston: Little, Brown, 1970.

Dobler, Lavinia G. *Great Rulers of the African Past*. New York: Doubleday, 1965.*

Drewel, Henry John, and John Pemberton III. *Yoruba: Nine Centuries of African Art and Thought*. New York: Center for African Art, 1989.

Elliott, K. *Benin: An African Kingdom and Culture*. Minneapolis: Lerner Publications, 1979.*

Equiano, Olaudah. *Equiano's Travels: The Interesting Narrative of the Life of Olaudah Equiano or Gustavas Vassa, the African*. New York: Praeger, 1967.

Harris, Joseph E. *Africans and their History*. New York: New American Library, 1987.

Joseph, Joan. *Black African Empires*. Franklin Watts, Inc., 1974.*

Kennerly, Karen. *The Slave Who Bought His Freedom.* New York: Dutton, 1971.*

Ki-Zerbo, Joseph. *Die Geschichte Schwarz-Afrikas.* [*The History of Black Africa*]. Wuppertal: Peter Hammer, 1979.

Kwamena-Poh, Michael. *African History in Maps.* London: Longman, 1982.

Larungu, Rute. *Myths and Legends From Ghana for African-American Cultures.* Telcraft Books, 1992.*

Law, Robin. *The Slave Coast of West Africa, 1550–1750.* New York: Oxford University Press, 1991.

Lystad, R, A. *The Ashanti: A Proud People.* Rutgers University Press, 1958.

McEvedy, Collin. *The Penguin Atlas of African History.* London: Penguin Books, 1980.*

Murray, Jocelyn. *Cultural Atlas of Africa.* New York: Facts On File, Inc., 1989.*

Newton, Alex. *West Africa—A Travel Survival Kit.* Australia: Lonely Planet Publications, 1992.

Oliver, Roland. *The African Experience.* New York: HarperCollins, 1991.

Oliver, Roland, and J.D. Fage. *A Short History of Africa.* 6th ed. London: Penguin Books, 1988.

Smith, R. S. *Kingdoms of the Yoruba.* University of Wisconsin Press, 1988.

Stacey, Tom. *Peoples of the Earth*. Tom Stacey and Europa, 1972.*

Stride, G. T., and C. Ifeka. *Peoples and Empires of West Africa*. New York: Africana Publishing, 1971.

Thompson, Elizabeth Bartlett. *Africa Past and Present*. Boston: Houghton Mifflin, 1966.

Wyndham, John. *Myths of Ife*. London: E. Macdonald, 1921.

Index

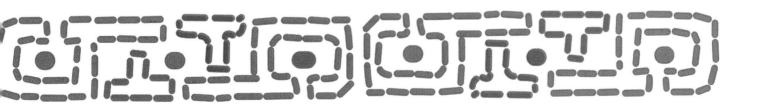

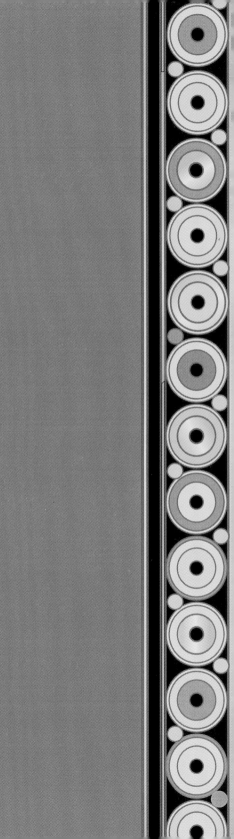

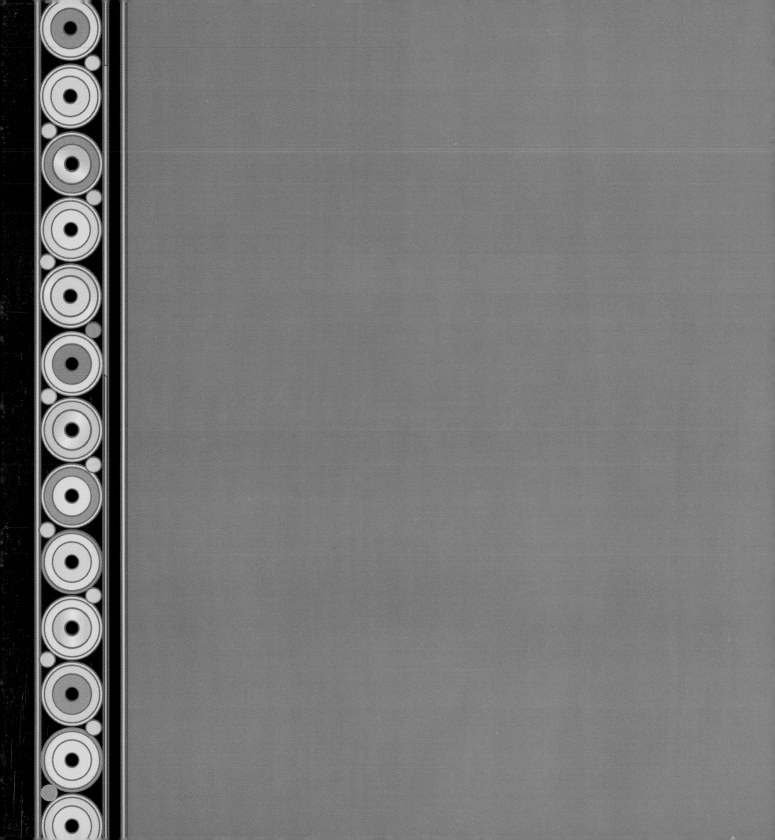